The Wedding That Almost Wasn't

The Wedding That Almost Wasn't

DONNA HAUGER

E-Book ISBN: 979-8-9935566-3-5
Paperback ISBN: 979-8-9935566-4-2
Hardback ISBN: 979-8-9935566-5-9

Dedication

To Cheri and Derek,
To Brian and Kari,
To Claire, William, Lucy, and Jack

May your lives always be guided by love, resilience, and the
courage to begin again.

Epigraph

"Memory is the diary we all carry about with us."
— Oscar Wilde

Contents

Part III: Journeys and Crossroads

Prologue

The quiet of Minnesota evenings feels different now. From the apartment above my son's garage, I hear the laughter of grandchildren drifting through the yard, the hum of daily life carrying on below. My husband's Parkinson's has changed the pace of our days, slowing us, reminding us of the fragility and strength that coexist in every season of life. Retirement has given me time to reflect, and in these moments of stillness, I find myself looking back.

Resilience. That's the word I keep coming back to. I didn't know it as a girl growing up in the 1940s, pumping water and reading by kerosene lamp. I just knew we got things done. My grandparents crossed an ocean with nothing but hope. My parents worked hard, quietly, without complaint. That strength stuck with me. It followed me into classrooms smelling of chalk dust and formaldehyde, into the joys and impact of teaching, into marriage, motherhood, and every twist and turn in between.

This memoir isn't about endings. It's about beginnings—how the life you start with shapes the life you live. To understand how I got here—wife, mother, teacher, caregiver—we need to go back. Back to the farm. Back to chores and dreams. Back to the girl who learned strength before she even realized she would need it.

Because much later, that strength would be tested again—on a day I never could have imagined, when my future almost slipped away. But that part comes later. For now, let's go back to the beginning.

PART I: ROOTS AND WINTERS

"The land is where our story begins, and memory is the harvest we keep."
— Anonymous

Life began in the rhythm of the seasons, where soil and snow shaped both play and sorrow. These early years were a harvest of innocence, grounding me in traditions, resilience, and the quiet wonder of farm life.

A Cry in Winter: The Threads That Stitch Us

The farm was my first universe—a patchwork of fields and seasons, blended together by the daily rhythms of work and play. I was born into its quiet expanse, where winter winds rattled the windows and summer sun baked the soil into dust. Childhood unfolded among treehouses and snowy days, laughter echoing across the fields, and sorrow buried beneath apple trees. Even then, life carried both fragility and wonder: the breathless nights of illness, the warmth of worship, the feasts that marked holidays. These early memories became the roots that held me fast, even as horizons far beyond the farm began to call.

The winter of 1944 pressed down hard on Fergus Falls, Minnesota—snow piled against windows, the air sharp enough to sting. On January 17, I arrived, woven into the unfolding tapestry of human experience of Thelma and Arnold Flatin. Our farm sat three miles south of Rothsay, a town so small you could miss it if you blinked, sixty miles from Fargo where the prairie stretched wide and endless.

Mom was the oldest of four, with dreams of becoming a hairdresser in Minneapolis, dreams cut short by homesickness. Her hearing was poor from childhood infections, so we learned to speak loudly, sometimes repeating ourselves until she caught the words. Later, when she wore hearing aids with a battery pack strapped to her chest, she laughed at how suddenly the world seemed noisy: refrigerator whirring, water boiling on the stove, crickets chirping.

∗ ∗ ∗

Long before I was born, Mom and Dad's story began at a basket social. I heard it so many times around the kitchen table that I can almost see it myself. Women packed suppers into boxes, men bid for them, and somewhere between laughter and competition Dad won more than a meal—he won Mom.

I wasn't there, but I the story became part of me. I can almost smell the bread and hear the gavel. That basket social was more than a meal—it was the beginning of the family I was born into, the thread that stitched me into their lives.

The church basement smelled of coffee and fried chicken, the kind of scent that clung to coats and hymnals long after the gathering ended. Long tables lined the room, each covered with boxes wrapped in gingham cloth or tied with ribbon, the women's suppers hidden inside like secrets waiting to be discovered.

Men jostled and teased one another, their voices rising above the hum of conversation. "Don't let Johnson outbid you again!" someone called, and laughter rippled through the crowd. Dad stood near the back, his hands shoved into his pockets, eyes scanning the boxes as though he were choosing more than a meal.

When the bidding began, the room grew louder, the

cadence of numbers and names bouncing off the walls. Dad's voice cut through—steady, determined—as he lifted his hand. The auctioneer's gavel tapped, and the box was his. He carried it to a table, setting it down with a kind of reverence. Mom sat nearby, cheeks flushed pink, her eyes darting between him and the box.

When he lifted the lid, the smell of fresh bread and roasted chicken filled the air. He glanced at her, a smile tugging at the corner of his mouth.

"Well," he said softly, "looks like I won more than supper tonight."

She laughed, shy but certain, and in that moment the basket became more than food—it became a promise, the first thread in the tapestry of their life together.

✳ ✳ ✳

Dad, oldest of six, attended a boarding school called the West Central School of Agriculture in Morris, MN, a University of Minnesota institution that trained young men in farming. He came home with calloused hands and a head full of plans, investing in land near his parents' farm—the land that became my childhood home.

As I grew, the world around me was shaped not just by the land we lived on, but by the people who carried us there—two families rooted in Norway, their branches reaching across oceans and generations. To understand my childhood, you have to understand the heritage that lived beneath it.

Our family's roots stretched across the Atlantic long before I understood what that meant. Grandpa Hanson left Sleneset, Norway at sixteen, turning his back on the sea because he knew it could never support him. My maternal great-grandfather made a similar choice, leaving the farmland outside Oslo for a patch of earth he could finally call his own. Growing up, I didn't fully grasp the courage it must have taken—I only knew our story began with people who refused to stay where life limited them.

Grandma and Grandpa Hanson brought with them a quiet Norwegian reserve, a love of open spaces, and a work ethic that settled over our family like weather. "Work first, talk later," Grandpa would say, not unkindly but as if he were reciting a law of nature. I can still picture him: shoulders squared, hands rough from labor, speaking in that clipped, steady voice that made every word feel earned.

Those traits shaped more than our days—they shaped the land I grew up on and the way I learned to move through the world. The prairie wind bent the grass outside our windows, and in the same way, their values bent us toward steadiness, responsibility, and a kind of strength that didn't need announcing. It was simply who we were.

Grandpa had been the son of a fisherman, but he always said the sea offered beauty, not security. So he traded waves for soil, a decision that still echoed through our family long after the salt had left his boots.

***

The values Grandma and Grandpa brought from Norway settled into the life of their Rothsay house—not just in the way they lived, but in the way the house itself felt. Every visit began with the warm spice of Grandma's fresh ginger cookies drifting through the kitchen. She let me dip them into her coffee, the cup warm between my hands, the sweet-bite of ginger softening in the milky brown liquid. Even now, that smell can pull me straight back into her doorway.

The house hummed with the quiet industry of her days. In one corner stood the old mangle ironer, its wooden rollers polished by years of use. When I was small, I watched her crank it by hand, guiding damp sheets and pillowcases through its heated press until they came out smooth and warm. Later she replaced it with an electric one, but the rhythm of ironing—that soft hiss of steam, the weight of the cast-iron heater on the stove, the careful smoothing of cloth—never changed.

On winter nights, she warmed bricks on top of the wood stove, wrapping them in towels before tucking them at the foot of the bed. It was the kind of quiet care she never spoke about, but you felt it when you slid your feet under the covers and found that unexpected pocket of heat.

To us kids, the house was both sanctuary and playground. Its rooms—some rented out like a small hotel—created a maze of hallways, half-closed doors, and hidden corners. My younger brother, Gary and I treated it as our private world.

We played hide-and-seek until the day he locked himself inside a wardrobe, his muffled cries turning my stomach cold. When we finally pried the door open, he tumbled out pale and wide-eyed. "I thought I'd never get out," he gasped.

Gary's wardrobe scare didn't stop us from exploring. If anything, it made the house feel even more mysterious. And nothing in that maze of rooms tugged at my curiosity more than the attic.

The stairs to Grandma's attic creaked under my weight, each step a warning that I was trespassing into a place half-forbidden, half-sacred. The air grew cooler as I climbed, tinged with the smell of dust and cedar. When I pushed open the narrow door, sunlight slanted through a small window, catching the motes that drifted like tiny spirits in the air.

The attic, with its unfinished beams, was my treasure cave—a jungle of trunks, their lids heavy with age. I ran my fingers across worn leather handles and cool metal clasps, feeling as though each one guarded a secret. When Grandma joined me, her steps slow but sure, she lifted the lid of a quilt trunk. The lift-out drawer held deer-skin gloves, a fur muff, and small valuables: coins, keys, cuff links, tie clips, rings. The fabric inside smelled faintly of earth and soap, stitched from old suits whose seams carried the weight of men's labor. Scattered among them were mothballs, sharp and pungent.

"Is that... mothballs?" I asked, wrinkling my nose. "Yes," Grandma replied. "They keep the moths and mice away."

Her words stirred a memory I had been told many times.

When I was two, I had rummaged through one of Mom's drawers, where she too had tucked mothballs among the linens. To my toddler eyes, the white pellets looked like candy. I ran to the kitchen, triumphant. "Mommy, I found candy! Yummy!" I squealed. Panic flashed across her face. "Spit it out!" she cried, prying at my mouth. Moments later, Dad was summoned, and the four of us — Mom, Dad, my baby brother, and me—rushed to the Fergus Falls hospital. I remember little, but the story was retold often: the tube slid down my throat, the suction that emptied my stomach, the relief when it was over.

The incident never stopped Mom from using mothballs. Mothballs remained part of our household, tucked among wool blankets, suits, and coats. Some even hung in containers in our closet. Years later, mom stored valuables in a cedar chest, rather than using mothballs because our clothing was made of synthetic fabrics, rather than fibers moths preferred. She and Dad gave me a cedar "hope chest," a symbol of a young woman's future. Mine was filled with linens and household items, waiting for the day I would leave home.

Back in Grandma's attic, the trunk before us held its own promises. After removing the drawer, Grandma looked at me with a quiet certainty. "Donna," she said, "this quilt will be yours one day. And the sewing kit too." Her words settled over me like a promise, and suddenly the attic felt less like storage and more like inheritance.

I peered into another trunk—embroidered linens folded with care, immigration papers yellowed at the edges, uniforms from both World Wars. I touched the brass buttons, imagining the men who had worn them, their lives stitched into the fabric of history.

For me, the attic was more than a room. It was a vault of memory, a place where the past waited patiently to be discovered. Each trunk held not just objects but stories, and each story seemed to whisper: *You belong to this lineage. You are part of this thread.*

Music filled Grandma and Grandpa Hanson's house just as surely as the smell of ginger cookies or the creak of the attic stairs. The upright piano stood against the wall, its keys yellowed from years of hymns and winter evenings. I pressed them unevenly, the melody stumbling out of my fingers. "Oh, Mom, can I practice later?" I'd plead, knowing full well that "later" rarely arrived.

She would only smile, sit beside me, and play by ear—her hands confident where mine faltered. In the lamplight our voices rose together, imperfect but earnest, a small chorus forged from patience and love. I didn't realize then that those evenings weren't just about learning music; they were teaching me how to find a rhythm with the people I loved, how to stay in tune even when the notes were hard.

On Dad's side, the music took on a different shape. My paternal grandmother lived just a mile away from our farm with her unmarried daughter. Grandpa had died young, leaving behind a quiet house that seemed to lean a little on the people inside it. My memories there are blurred at the edges, but I remember the days when Grandma hosted her church circle. Her parlor filled with women—coats steaming from the cold, voices warming the room before the coffee even finished brewing.

I sat at the piano again, fingers stumbling through hymns while their laughter, stories, and prayers drifted behind me. They spoke of children and crops, of heartaches and hope, weaving a net of support that carried them through harsh winters and harder years. At the time, I believed I was simply offering background music. Looking back, I understand I was witnessing the quiet, steady power of women who kept each other upright, one gathering at a time.

Winter pressed against every wall of our lives, teaching us how to endure: the hauling of wood to the stove, the quilts stacked so heavy they almost pinned us to bed, the ice you learned to step on gently lest it betray you. But winter also revealed warmth—voices rising around a piano, coffee steaming in Grandma's parlor, laughter thawing what the cold tried to claim. Those were the seasons that taught me that survival takes grit, but joy takes intention.

Roots in the Soil

Those lessons carried into every season. Joy was not only found in music and laughter but in the ordinary rituals of farm life—the chores, the meals, the animals, and the endless cycle of work that linked each day together. If winter taught us endurance, the farm itself taught us how to live in time.

We lived on 280 acres, anchored by a large red barn, a clay silo, a granary elevated above the ground to protect the grain from pests, a chicken coop built of scrap lumber and a one-bedroom farmhouse. All four of us—Mom, Dad, Gary, and me—slept upstairs in one large room above the kitchen and living room. Winter nights brought the scurry of mice in the walls. Dad set snap traps, baited with peanut butter, in hopes of catching the predators. Dealing with the mouse droppings and keeping the critters out of our cupboards, furniture and the clothing was a struggle. Life on the farm carried its own set of challenges indoors and out.

Ice crept across the inside of our windows, so thick Gary and I would scrape it with a fingernail to create intricate designs, shapes, and write our names. It was our natural "Etch-A-Sketch." Dad stretched plastic over the panes in some rooms like the bedroom, but the drafts still whispered through. If winter brought ice to the windows, summer brought its own discomforts.

✳ ✳ ✳

Our outhouse, a small shed-like structure built over a deep, dark hole, sat north of the house, far enough to keep the smell at bay but close enough for convenience. Two wooden seats with lids—one large, one annoyingly small for a child's bottom—tried to keep the flies out, though in summer their constant, pervasive buzzing filled the small space. I always wondered how many more pests like spiders were waiting in places where they couldn't be spotted, like under the lid. The decomposition of urine and human waste produced a foul odor of rotten eggs that I detested. It was a pungent, thick smell that seemed to cling to my clothes long after I left. In the summer, the smell intensified with sweat running down my back.

"Hold your breath and hurry," I muttered each time, reaching for the "reading material"—a stack of old Sears, Roebuck catalogs and a Farmer's Almanac hanging from a nail, its corner pre-punched for convenience. The pages were slick and stiff, requiring a good crumpling before they were even remotely usable. I preferred instead the little white, blue speckled porcelain enamel potty tucked in the bedroom corner. It felt like safety, like a secret escape from the dreaded shed. The outhouse was necessity; the potty was comfort.

Even now, I can still feel the relief of choosing the small metal refuge over the buzzing dark of that summer shack, or the freezing, shuddering winter trips where I'd run back to the house with snow packed inside my shoes.

Every Halloween, the threat of the outhouse being tipped over by local pranksters hung in the air. We lived in fear of coming out to find our familiar, smelly, wooden world lying on its side, or worse—finding it tipped while in use. Luckily, ours was never tipped, though I remember the stories of neighbors whose, as they say, "night soil" was left exposed to the world.

From the safety and routine of our home, we ventured outward, testing boundaries and tasting the wide-open freedom the prairie offered the moment we stepped outside.

Childhood meant roaming. Gary and I chased butterflies across pastures, plucked wildflowers for Mom, and raced down gullies carved by heavy rains. Our laughter echoed in the ditches, our shoes muddy and our knees scraped. Later, bicycles became our wings, rattling over bumpy ground, carrying us farther into the fields.

"Bet you can't catch me!" Gary shouted, pedaling hard. "Watch me," I yelled back, legs pumping, the prairie wind in my hair.

Freedom was measured in distance from the house and the thrill of returning just before supper.

When we weren't chasing the wind across the fields, we spent time with the people who carried our family's history—our grandparents, each with their own world waiting for us, shaping our sense of family, history, and belonging.

The same land that gave us freedom in summer demanded endurance in winter. Winter arrived like a thing that settled into the house—white on the windows, a weight on the quilts, a slow hardening of the world outside. We never thought of it as hardship; it was simply the way things were. Dad's ax was the first sound most mornings: wood split, a stove fed, a life kept warm.

My brother and I raced from our bunk beds to the kitchen, fingers numb, to wait in the halo of heat where the stove made the room smell of sap and smoke. Nights were layered with quilts my mother and grandmother had stitched from old suits; in the morning the edges of the windowpanes were crusted with frosty lace and the house held its breath until the fire lived again.

The fire fed us, but water—and how we gathered it—kept our daily lives in motion.

Water had to be asked for, coaxed out of the ground. The pump by the sink needed priming—a spill of water, then the up-and-down movement of the handle until a thin, cold stream surrendered itself into the bucket. We hauled kettles to the stove and watched steam rise as if the day could be boiled into being.

The underground cistern and the windmill were household characters in their own right: one stored summer rain in patient darkness, the other creaked and sang in the wind as it lifted water for animals and fields. Rainwater slid down the gutters into the cistern for washing and cleaning, while the windmill's blades turned tirelessly to draw water from the well for the barn and garden. Together they kept our days moving.

With that came tradition, none more memorable than Saturday nights. Before Dad finally rigged a shower in the old shanty—an old jail he'd purchased for the seasonal hired hands—cleanliness was a simpler, sharper business. In the summer, we had a "miracle" of gravity and a sun-warmed tank on the windmill, while in spring and fall, we either accepted the galvanized tub in the kitchen by the stove or the sharp, shivering embrace of freezing running water. Living in Minnesota in winter, there was simply no choice once the water froze.

With water drawn from the pump, our Saturday nights became a ritual of cleansing, laughter, and the measured order of bath time. The whole house seemed to prepare for it like a performance. The big galvanized tub was dragged into the kitchen, its metal sides clanging against the floorboards. Kettles of scalding water lined up on the stove like actors waiting in the wings, each one steaming and hissing as if impatient for its cue.

We climbed in and out in a practiced order—youngest first, father last—the water turning darker as the week's chores and play were stripped away. I hated being second in line; Gary always got the first dip, splashing in the clean warmth while I waited, shivering, for my turn. By the time I climbed in, the water had cooled and carried the faint grit of farm dust. Still, I lingered, stretching my toes against the curved tin, pretending I was floating in a secret lake.

The kitchen glowed with kerosene lamplight, shadows

trembling across the walls. Splashes echoed against tin and wood, and the air smelled of soap and steam. Mom's homemade soap—rendered fat and lye—was sharp and earthy, a scent that belonged only to Saturday nights. She scrubbed us briskly, her hands firm, as though she could wash away not just dirt but mischief.

Dad's turn came last, his broad shoulders filling the tub, the water sloshing dangerously close to the rim. By then, the bath had become more ritual than cleansing, a weekly ceremony that reminded us we were a family bound by habit and necessity.

When it was over, the tub was emptied with a splash into the yard, steam rising into the night air. We scampered upstairs, skin pink and clean, hair damp, heavy quilts on our beds waiting. The house smelled faintly of soap and kerosene, and I always felt a quiet satisfaction—as though Saturday night had reset the week, leaving us ready to begin again.

When our baths were done and we were tucked beneath the heavy quilts, there was always a sense of settling, as if the whole house were exhaling. Saturday night had its own kind of ceremony, but it was really all in preparation for Sunday—the day that waited quietly on the other side of sleep, polished and set apart from the rest of the week.

Sundays on the farm never belonged to the week that came before or the one waiting just ahead. They were suspended days, quiet and hushed, as if someone had turned down the volume on the whole countryside. Even the barn seemed to breathe more slowly. We dressed in our Sunday best—bright white stockings that never stayed white long, dresses with petticoats that rustled when I walked, and the little white gloves I could never quite keep clean. Mom wore her patent leather shoes that clicked sharply against the kitchen linoleum, and Dad and Gary were transformed with suits, bow ties, and shoes polished so brightly you could almost see your face in them.

At church we claimed a pew near the back, close enough to hear the sermon but far enough that Mom could keep an eye on Gary and me. After the opening hymn, we were sent off to Sunday School, where Bible stories came alive in basements that smelled faintly of chalk dust and sugar cookies. While we colored pictures of Noah's Ark, Mom and Dad drifted downstairs to visit with the neighbors—grown-up talk that floated through the hallways like a steady, comforting hum.

By the time church let out, the day had settled into its proper shape. Stores were closed—by law, by custom, by the understanding that Sunday was set apart—and the farm tasks waited patiently for Monday. At home the kitchen filled with the warmth of a big Sunday dinner: roast or ham, mashed potatoes whipped smooth, gravy that simmered all morning, whatever vegetables were in season, and always dessert. We ate slowly, as if stretching the hours themselves.

The rest of the afternoon unfolded gently. Sometimes we visited grandparents; sometimes the grandparents visited us. Sometimes we simply rested—reading, talking quietly, or doing nothing at all, which on a farm felt like a kind of luxury. Sundays were a pause button, a reminder that life wasn't only chores and school and work. It was also being together, respecting tradition, and marking time in a way that made the whole week feel anchored. But even the quietest Sunday couldn't hold off the week for long.

Monday was laundry day, and the whole house seemed to orbit around it like planets circling a steamy sun. The kitchen filled with fog so thick the windows wept, and the air smelled of soap and wet cloth. I learned to read the rhythm of it: the scrape of the washboard, the hiss of boiling water, the heavy *thwack* of the wringer as fabric surrendered its weight.

Mom shaved slivers of homemade soap with a knife, the curls dissolving into the pot like snowflakes melting on a tongue. I loved watching them vanish, the water turning cloudy and strong. My job was small—fetching buckets, stirring, sometimes daring to plunge my hands into the hot suds until Mom scolded, "You'll scald yourself!" Still, I liked the sting, proof that I was part of the work.

The wringer fascinated me. Its rollers groaned as shirts and sheets slid through, dripping and flattened, as if the machine had squeezed the life out of them. I'd sneak a finger close, just to feel the pull, until Mom's sharp voice cut through the steam: "Keep your hands back, Doni!" Mom's softening of the Donna Lou my Aunt Gina had chosen—always sounded more like me. I obeyed, but the thrill of danger lingered.

Outside, the clotheslines stretched across the yard like a horizon of flags. On windy days, they snapped and billowed, a parade of our family's labor. My brother and I ran beneath them, ducking between sheets that slapped my face, "Can't catch me," I'd yell, teasing my brother and laughing as though the laundry was playing tag with us. In winter, the garments froze stiff, standing like soldiers propped against chairs until the stove thawed them back into softness.

Laundry day was more than soap and steam—it was a ritual of transformation. Dirt and sweat became clean cloth, heavy buckets became lines of laundry lifting in the breeze. The wringer washer saved mom from having to no longer lug wet clothes around. The ordinary became a kind of magic. I didn't know it then, but those Mondays taught me something lasting: that care could be measured in small, repeated acts, and that love often arrived disguised as work.

Once clothes were clean and dried, the work of feeding the family began, each meal a new ritual.

* * *

Dinners and suppers were more than meals; they were rituals that interwove the week together. By late morning, the kitchen was alive with sound and scent. The wood stove glowed hot, its belly humming while Mom bent over pots and pans like a quiet general directing her troops. The air filled with the fragrance of roasting meat—sometimes chicken, sometimes goose, sometimes a beef roast—all from our own farm. Dad butchered whatever was needed, making use of nearly every part of the animal, even the blood. During butchering season, Mom prepared *blodklubb*,

Norwegian blood dumplings made from blood with potatoes, pork, and flour added, served with butter and bacon or fried crisp for breakfast the next morning. I ate *blodklubb* eagerly, savoring the dense, earthy dumpling with its crusty edges and buttery sheen. Then one day I learned what gave it its dark, almost purplish color—blood. The word alone made the richness turn strange in my mouth. My fork hovered, then fell to the plate, and though I never ate it again, the memory of that moment stayed with me, a reminder of how quickly delight can shift to unease.

Nothing went to waste. Gizzards, livers, and hearts of hens were common fare. I always hoped the serving plate of chicken would pass me first so I could snatch the gizzard—chewy and tough from its muscular texture. The hearts were tender, but I left the liver for others; its flavor was too gamey for me.

Vegetables came straight from the garden, their colors bright against worn enamel bowls: carrots slick with butter, beans snapped fresh that morning, potatoes mashed until smooth and steaming. Another favorite was *klubb*, Norwegian potato dumplings made from grated raw potatoes, flour, salt, and bits of pork, simmered in salted water and topped with butter and sugar. Leftovers were fried for breakfast, their crunchy edges a treat.

The table itself became a stage. Plates clattered, silverware chimed, and the smell of bread—yeasty, golden, still warm from the oven—drifted through the house. I hovered near the pie, its crust bubbling at the edges, apples inside soft and syrupy, promising a sweet finish. Dad carved the meat with slow precision, his knife glinting in the lamplight, while Gary and I fidgeted, waiting for our portions. Mom's voice reminded us to fold our hands and bow our heads. Grace was spoken simply but carried weight: gratitude for food, for family, for the work that had brought it all to the table. At times, Mom would share a Norwegian prayer.

I understood more Norwegian than I spoke, since Mom and Dad used it when they wanted to keep secrets from us kids. My vocabulary was limited—"*Kan du snakke norsk?*" (Can you speak Norwegian?), "*litegrann*" (a little bit), and a few numbers—but the cadence of their words became familiar.

Conversation rose and fell like music—talk of chores, weather, neighbors, and plans for the week ahead. Laughter often broke out, sudden and bright, and I felt the warmth of belonging settle over me like another quilt. There was nothing fancy about those meals, but they tasted of place and people. Every bite carried the pulse of farm life: the soil that grew the vegetables, the animals we tended, the hands that churned butter and baked bread. Our family times were proof that ordinary work could become ceremony, that food could be both sustenance and celebration.

Beyond the table itself, the work of keeping food through the season carried its own kind of wonder. Storage and preservation felt like magic and promise. Knobby potatoes and carrots with dusty skins slept through the winter in our cool, dark root cellar in the basement. Its damp air smelled like earth from the dirt from the crawl space. Jars of watermelon, dill and sweet pickles, canned peaches, pears and applesauce lined the shelves in rows. Picking strawberries, blueberries and raspberries with sticky fingers was pure joy, and Mom turned those fruits into jam and jelly that lasted us through the winter months.

Making butter was a chore we worked on together. After the milk settled, we skimmed the cream into the churn and took turns working the wooden dasher up and down until the fat gathered into golden lumps and the buttermilk separated. We washed and patted the butter smooth with wooden paddles, sprinkled salt, and cut it into blocks that tasted sweet and creamy. At breakfast, the leftover buttermilk showed up in waffles and pancakes—fluffy, tangy, and always crowned with homemade maple syrup.

Ice cream was our family's collective labor of love. The tin can of cream, sugar, and vanilla sat inside a wooden bucket packed with ice and rock salt; my brother and I took turns turning the crank trading places to keep the motion steady. The dasher scraped, the mixture thickened, and after the can spent hours wrapped in salt and ice, we pried it open to a soft, cold sweetness that made hot days disappear. I still remember the thrill of that first spoonful—cold enough to sting my teeth, sweet enough to make me forget the work it took to get there.

Whether elaborate or everyday, food was always a measure of care. Simple things—bread warm from the stove, butter eaten before it reached the table, the slap of lids on jars—were how we measured care. The food kept us fed, but it also held memory: the turn of seasons, the work of hands, and the taste of a childhood that was built one meal at a time.

Preservation was more than survival—it was memory, ritual, and anticipation. Each jar, each block of butter, each slab of ice was a promise that the farm could carry us through the lean months. For me, it was also wonder: the idea that seasons could be captured, stored, and opened again when the world outside was gray.

And when the jars were sealed and the last churn scraped clean, the house settled into its own kind of keeping. Evening gathered around us, and the light that carried us through those hours came from the kerosene lamps swinging above the kitchen table, casting amber halos where we did homework by hand. We learned to read in that glow, the printed page flaring every time the wind made the wick tremble. The light felt like an insistence: learn now, while there's a chance.

"Hold it closer," Mom would say when my book drooped. "Don't burn the page," Dad warned, tapping the lamp as if to steady both flame and child. And when the snow piled outside, blanketing the world in white, that light became our small, determined sun, inside and out.

But morning always carried us beyond the lamplight, out to the animals whose needs shaped the rhythm of our days.

Stepping into the Day

Of course, much of what fed us began with the animals we tended each day. Chickens pecked and muttered in a bare, wire-fenced yard, dust rising as they clawed for grain. Their coop was a straw-stuffed room of nesting boxes and low roosts; a kerosene lantern hummed at dusk while hens settled and fussed. I fed them cracked corn and kitchen scraps, fetched eggs each morning, and learned candling—sorting and sizing the eggs for market—keeping the rejects in our pantry for breakfasts and baking. I loved the soft cluck of hens as I reached beneath them, though sometimes they pecked my fingers in protest, reminding me that even small creatures had their pride. Chicks were kept warm under a heat lamp until their feathers came in. A rooster's cry split the dawn and set the day in motion.

The geese were louder, bolder. They marched the yard in a honking line, wings outstretched, flapping menacingly, like sentinels ready to defend their territory. More than once they rushed me, their beaks snapping, and I'd squeal and dash for the porch, half-terrified, half-delighted at their noisy defiance. They were watchdogs in feathered disguise, as useful as they were menacing. Our geese were also meat for a holiday dinner, often with a turkey, purchased from a turkey farmer.

Our hogs were kept in a sty in our old red barn that had a smaller lean-to room tacked onto the south side. The roof of this addition was lower, slanting down as if taking a bow to the main structure. Perched on the highest point of the main roof, was an old black, wrought-iron weather vane, a silhouette of a rooster. It's metal frame creaking as it spun. Watching the breeze, it was always showing us which was the wind was blowing. The pigs had a cozy, straw bedded floor inside, but a door led out to a muddy, churned-up area they endlessly rooted with their snouts, creating a dark, wet mess. Feed, consisting of food scraps and grains would be scattered on ground and placed in wooden troughs. When the sows had piglets, often they would be seen lying together in piles to keep warm or rooting in the mud. A simple wooden fence kept them enclosed.

Sows grunted while piglets squealed, clustering for warmth. Sometimes, a sow would have a runt piglet who was not getting enough nourishment. I would take the piglet into the house and nurse it with a bottle of warm milk, its tiny mouth tugging greedily until it learned to eat from a pan.

We raised hogs for pork, bacon, and my favorite—salted pig's feet, jarred and ready without need of refrigeration. There was a lot of bone and cartilage on the feet, so I had to gnaw on the bones and chew the meat and skin from them, similar to how I ate around a chicken wing.

The 1940s included the tail end of the Great Depression and the rationing years of World War II. Being frugal was a necessity to survive living on the farm. Waste was uncommon. Mom used all parts of the hog. Making head cheese (called *sylte* in Norwegian), was a practical and popular menu item especially for lunch. Preparing it involved boiling the hog's head minus the eyes and brains until the meat falls off the bone (about 3 hours) chopping finely, and straining the broth. Return meat to broth and season well. Simmer until thick, then pour into loaf pans. Chill until firm—slice and serve cold on sandwiches with mustard, mayonnaise, or pickles.

Raising hogs meant food for the table, but to me they were also creatures of stubborn personality—curious, messy, and oddly endearing.

Black and white Holstein dairy cows lived in the barn with straw for beds. Their steady, warm breath of animals rising against the winter cold. Dad rose early to move fresh, earthy smelling alfalfa from the hayloft and pleasant vinegary corn silage from the silo into the long, low mangers located in front of the cows' stalls for feed. Twice a day, he milked the cows; in warmer months the herd moved out to graze, guided by our collie, Shep, along the fenced path under the road to the slough—a wide, quiet stretch of water, almost a small lake. I never knew for sure what fed it; maybe a spring deep underground, maybe just the rains that gathered there year after year.

In the spring and summer, my brother and I joined Shep in the rain. Clothed in our slick raincoats, umbrella's in hand, side by side, we dashed through the gentle rain, puddles splashing beneath our hurried steps. Our laughter cut through the quiet, a private moment as we ran the familiar path leading to the slough and our grazing cattle.

The barnyard was always a busy, living place—its black earth churned with cattle manure and the thick, unmistakable smell that came with it. In spring and summer, the heat only intensified the sharp bite of ammonia and hydrogen sulfide in the air. It wasn't pleasant, but it meant the work of the season had begun.

Dad used that manure to bring life back into our corn, wheat, rye, soybean, and flax fields. Before tractors came along, he would hitch one of our steady work horses to the manure spreader and guide it across the freshly turned soil. Afterward, he'd harness another horse to the disk harrow, the blades clattering as they mixed the manure into the earth and smoothed the surface for seed.

Those horses did everything—plowing and cultivating the fields, mowing the hay, and pulling wagons loaded with grain—until the day Dad brought home a small Allis-Chalmers tractor. Even then, the cycles of the seasons stayed the same. Every fall, the fields were ploughed under, and by spring they were ready again for planting. Each year the crop rotated, giving every section of land a chance to rest and renew.

Calving came in spring. Calves were my companions in those spring days. I loved holding out my hand for them to suckle; their mouths closed around my fingers, perhaps mistaking them for a salt block, or simply offering affection. Their tongues, rough with backward-facing papillae, tugged gently, while the warmth of their breath and the soft nudges of their noses filled me with a quiet peace—a reminder that even amid chores, the farm offered moments of companionship.

As animals marked my days, the fields marked my

summers. Summer fields smelled of sweet green and sunbaked dust when the alfalfa came up. The mower moved slowly, pulled by a team of horses, and the cut rows lay like seams across the land until the rakes gathered them into windrows, long narrow rows, to dry. We shoved pitchforks into warm, fragrant hay and tossed handfuls onto the wagon until it rose like a rolling hill.

Once, I ran into a pitchfork left in the grass; a tine sliced my leg and the blood ran until Mom wrapped it with a cloth. The scar above my ankle still remembers that day.

When thunderstorms threatened, the whole world sped up. Men shouted, horses strained, and we scrambled to get the hay under the barn roof before rain turned it to weighty rot.

We rode the loaded wagon, jumped into the stack to tamp it down, and felt the ropes pull the hay up into the loft with a clanging, heart pounding rhythm that tasted like danger and freedom.

Up in the hayloft the light was a slow show of sunbeams and dust. Hay spread below like a warm, lurching ocean—soft where you landed, sharp where it scraped your skin. We swung from the tow rope, side to side, until our hands blistered, sampled a stray bit of straw that tasted of dry earth, and laughed at the muffled sounds of the barn animals beneath us.

The ropes bit our palms, the wood smelled of sweat and oil, and when you dove into a pile of hay you felt, for a wild, perfect second, like the barn belonged to you.

But the barn was more than a playground; it was also

where the day's real work began. Dad milked on a three-legged stool, knees spread, a pail cupped between his legs while the barn smelled of straw and warm milk. Each cow had a stall and a name in the way he spoke to them; I remember slipping my small hand under a warm udder, learning the flow, and giggling as I squirted milk into the waiting mouth of a barn cat. Those early lessons felt like initiation—work that made you part of the place.

Then came the cream separator and the sharp surety of machinery. We used to crank it by hand until the disks spun cream from milk. One afternoon the machine ate the tip of my brother's finger. I can still see the white of bone and the slick of red; his scream cut the barn's usual sounds in half. Mom ran. Time seemed to fold around that single moment—panic, the hurried trip to the house, the heavy quiet afterward.

Milk was our livelihood, sold at market, but it also filled our glasses at supper and flavored the dishes on our table. The small room in our cool, dark cellar—tucked deep enough into the earth that the walls held a steady, natural chill—felt like the house's bank vault, heavy with the promise of paydays and preservation. It wasn't as cold as the icebox in the kitchen, where we kept slabs of ice, but it kept the milk safe until it was time to haul it up the steps and out into the world.

Upstairs we had other ways of keeping things cool. An insulated cupboard sat beside the stove, a wooden chest lined with tin that held a block of ice like a carved heart.

As it sweated, a slow drip filled a pan beneath it, and the cupboard breathed cold into our milk and butter.

In spring and fall, the iceman's truck would rattle down the gravel road; in winter, Dad cut great squares from the slough and hauled them home, the air smelling of wet earth and iron. Cold was something we managed the way we managed everything else: with work, cunning, and an eye for what would keep.

"Make sure the pan's under it this time," Mom would call over the stove smoke. "Don't let it melt before supper," Dad joked, hefting a slab of ice like a small, heavy promise.

When the snow closed the road, the car slept by the highway and the horses woke. Dad hitched the cutter, wrapped the bench in quilts, and carried hot bricks from the stove to tuck at our feet. We rode across the white hush, wind slapping our faces, breath puffing like steam. Once the sleigh caught a rut and tipped; Mom sailed into a drift and lay on her back petrified, a sudden snow angel. That wobble between danger and laughter was everything I loved about winter then.

"Hold on tight!" Dad called as the sleigh lurched. Mom popped up, brushing snow from her hair, and laughed, "Well, that was more exciting than the highway!"

The Night the Barn Burned

Winter, spring, or summer—life on the farm held its share of sudden crises. When the barn burned from an electrical fault, neighbors arrived as if the farm were a single body and they, its hands. Men hauled timber, cut hay, and threshed grain; women set long tables in the yard and unloaded hot food.

The fire came like a living thing, sudden and merciless. One moment the barn hummed with its usual sounds—the shuffle of hooves, the creak of timbers—and the next, a sharp crack split the air. Flames licked upward, hungry and fast, turning wood into torches. The smell was acrid, a mix of burning hay and singed hair, thick enough to sting the back of my throat.

Smoke rolled out in heavy waves, swallowing the yard until the world shrank to a blur of orange and black. Sparks drifted upward into the night sky, wild stars rising to meet the constellations that watched silently overhead. The heat pressed against our skin like a furnace door swung open, forcing us back even as we tried to move forward.

Inside the haze, the animals panicked. Hooves hammered the ground, a frantic percussion against the dirt. Their cries—high, guttural, desperate—cut through the roar of flames. My father moved through that chaos with a strength I had never seen. His shirt clung to him with sweat and smoke, but adrenaline made him unstoppable. He ripped apart calf bins and stalls, splinters flying, iron hinges shrieking as they gave way. Each freed animal stumbled out into the night air, steam rising from their flanks as if the fire itself had branded them. I remember Bob Larson lifting my father's arm as if to say, *We've got this*, while a line of casseroles steamed on our kitchen steps, their savory scents mingling with the bitter smoke.

Time folded around that night—panic, rescue, exhaustion, and finally, the quiet aftermath. The barn stood blackened and broken, but the animals lived, and so did we. That day taught me what the farm meant beyond our fence: people showed up. The help wasn't charity so much as belonging—practical, blunt, and steady.

Looking back, I see the fire not only as destruction but as revelation. It showed me the force of my father, the tenacity of our animals, and the unspoken covenant of neighbors who showed up without being asked. Against the vast, indifferent prairie sky, the fire became a reminder: survival was never solitary. It was forged together by community, by hands that reached into the smoke, by voices that refused to let us stand alone.

By the time the barn was burning, there was never really a question of saving it. In the early 1950s, fire protection on a farm like ours was limited by distance, water, and time. We were three miles from Rothsay, beyond any hydrants, beyond any easy source of water. Our windmill drew just enough for daily life—cattle, washing, cooking—but nothing that could stand against a barn fire fed by dry hay and timber.

If the fire trucks came—and they almost certainly did—they would have come knowing that the barn was already lost. Volunteer firemen from town had to be called from their homes or fields, gather their equipment, and drive out on gravel roads. By then, the fire would have been doing what barn fires always did: climbing fast, roaring high, collapsing inward. There was no pond nearby to draft from, no creek running year-round, no reserve of water waiting to be tapped.

So the work would not have been about putting the fire out. It would have been about *holding the line*. Protecting the farmhouse came first. Then the granary, the garage, the chicken coop—buildings that could still be saved if the heat was kept back and the sparks knocked down. The silo, too, might have been watched carefully, its distance and construction offering a chance. The firemen would have positioned themselves where they could do the most good with what little water they had, wetting down roofs, knocking back embers, and making sure the fire did not leap from building to building.

That kind of firefighting doesn't leave the same impression as flames. It is quieter, more deliberate, and often happens after the most dramatic moment has already passed. What stays in my memory is the barn itself—burning, collapsing, gone—because that was the moment when something permanent disappeared. The rest are just memories of what remained.

The barn that replaced the one we lost was not a replica. It was longer, set on a new concrete foundation, with a rounded roof that rose smoothly instead of sharply, built to hold machines as much as animals. It was laid out for an electric barn cleaner that ran the length of the gutters, pulling waste away with the steady patience of a motor. Forks leaned idle more often after that. Painted a light yellow like the farmhouse, the new barn looked as though it belonged to a different time, even while standing in the same place.

The old barn had smelled of hay and manure, warm milk and leather, of dust rising when a door swung open. It creaked and settled as it cooled at night, the sounds of animals shifting, chains clinking, breath steaming in winter air. The work had its own music: the scrape of a shovel, the slap of milk into an open pail, the low voices of cows and people sharing the dark.

The new barn smelled cleaner—of concrete and metal, of disinfectant and cold. It sounded different too. Electric lights clicked on, ventilation fans pushed air through spaces that once held it close, and the barn cleaner hummed without pause. Milking no longer rang hollow in a pail. An automatic milker clipped to a cow's udder, moved milk through clear tubes into chilled bulk tanks housed in a separate milk room, sealed off and cool. The clatter of cans, the hauling and scrubbing, faded into memory. Milk waited now in stainless steel, held at temperature until it was taken away.

Everything about the work changed. Less backache.

Fewer scraped palms. A new order imposed by switches and motors instead of muscle and habit. There was relief in that, and gratitude. But there was also loss. The barn no longer breathed and spoke the way the old one had. It no longer creaked; it hummed. And in that steady sound was the knowledge that something familiar had ended, even as something easier had begun. But the barn was only a frame; the animals remained its heartbeat.

The animals were more than chores; they were companions, teachers, and sometimes mischief-makers. Each one carried its own pattern, its own place in the structure of our days.

Together, these creatures filled the farm with sound and motion—clucks, honks, grunts, lowing, barking. They were not just livestock; they were part of the flow of family life, shaping my childhood as surely as the land itself.

Daily chores gave our lives structure, but the seasons gave them shape. Just as animals marked the mornings and meals marked the days, the fields marked the years. And when August arrived, everything bent toward harvest—the land, the people, even the air itself.

The Season of Gathering

Harvest was not just another chore; it was the climax of the year, the moment when all the sweat of spring planting and summer tending revealed its reward. Every task before it—feeding animals, tending gardens, mending fences—was practice for this season of abundance. By mid-August that time meant harvest, and the air itself seemed heavy with grain and the farm moved to a single heartbeat: bring it in, store it, save it for winter.

The heads of wheat bent low, swollen with seed, stalks browned by the relentless sun. Dad worked the two-horse grain binder, the leather harness creaking as the horses pulled, their breath steaming even in the heat. The paddle pushed stalks into the bar, the canvas belt carrying them forward, twine snapping tight around each bundle before scattering them in neat rows across the field.

I remember the rhythm of it—six bundles gathered into shocks, stood upright like sentinels drying in the August blaze. My job was small then, carrying water jugs or chasing stray stalks, but I felt part of something larger. Dust clung to my skin, the smell of straw sharp in my nose, and the sound of the binder mixed with cicadas humming from the fence line.

When the grain was ready, we forked the bundles by hand onto the wagon, horses straining against the weight. Dad pitched them into the thresher powered by his Allis Chalmers tractor. The machine roared, swallowing the harvest in a cloud of dust, while the fan blew straw into a growing golden mound. Wagon after wagon carried grain to the granary, the air thick with sweat and grit.

Later, the thresher gave way to a combine, sleek and efficient, but in those early years harvest was muscle and teamwork. Looking back, I see how those days taught me endurance—the knowledge that abundance comes only through sweat, dust, and the steady flow of hands working together.

Harvest was muscle and dust in the fields, but in the farmhouse it was feast and fellowship. While Dad and the hired hands pitched bundles into the thresher, Mom orchestrated meals with the precision of a general and the generosity of a queen. Early breakfast, morning lunch, dinner at noon, afternoon lunch, and supper after chores—each one a ceremony of abundance.

Breakfast of baked ham, fried potatoes, eggs sunny-side-up, toasted homemade bread and oatmeal was ready after dad finished milking the cows. The aroma of fresh coffee filled the air. Cream and sugar was a must. By mid-morning, Mom carried sandwiches, pies, and coffee to the men in the field, her apron dusted with flour, her voice brisk but kind. I loved trailing behind her, balancing a plate or jug, watching the men pause in their labor to eat with gratitude that showed in every bite.

At the farmhouse, threshing dinners were legendary. The table groaned under platters of roast beef in gravy, golden-fried chicken, or hickory-smoked ham. Mountains of mashed potatoes gleamed with homemade butter, corn-on-the-cob steamed in bowls, carrots and beans glistened, and crisp lettuce with radishes added color. Warm breads came straight from the oven, their crusts crackling as knives sliced through. Pickles, relishes, jams, and jellies lined the table like jewels.

Desserts were the perfect finale to the meal: strawberry, apple, raisin, pumpkin, lemon, and mincemeat pies, their crusts still warm. Cakes with thick frosting stood tall beside plates of cookies, and sometimes homemade ice cream appeared, its cold sweetness a miracle after hours of heat and dust. And always, coffee bubbled in the percolator, its aroma filling the house like a steady drumbeat of hospitality.

When additional help was needed to get the harvest in, neighbors gathered shoulder to shoulder, their laughter rising above the clatter of forks and the scrape of chairs. Children darted between tables, sneaking cookies when mothers weren't looking, while men leaned back in their chairs, sighing with satisfaction before heading out again. I remember standing on a stool to dry dishes, my hands wrinkled from hot water, listening to the hum of voices that seemed to stitch the room together.

For me, those meals were more than food. They were proof that harvest was not endured alone. The work in the fields demanded sweat and stamina, but the meals reminded us of joy, of community, of the way abundance was meant to be shared.

The day I was tall enough to reach the pedals on the tractor, my world shifted. Until then, my jobs had been small—carrying water jugs, chasing stray stalks, helping

Mom in the kitchen. But when Dad waved me over, his voice half-serious and half-proud, I felt the ground tilt toward something new.

"Think you can handle her?" he asked, one hand resting on the tractor fender, the other steady on his hip.

The machine roared beneath me, the seat vibrating against my legs, the smell of oil and earth rising with the exhaust. My hands gripped the wheel, knuckles white, as Dad gave a quick nod. I pressed the pedal, awkward at first, the tractor lurching forward like a beast testing its rider. Fear and exhilaration tangled in my chest, but I held on, determined not to falter under his watchful eye.

As the rows of corn stretched ahead, the blades cut through soil with a steady hum, drowning out every other sound. Dust rose in golden clouds, clinging to my skin, while the sun pressed hot against my shoulders. Sometimes I wore my bathing suit, hoping the sun would bronze me, though as a redhead it only left freckles and pink skin. I laughed at myself, but kept trying, the tractor seat scorching against my legs.

Steering became a game in my head: one row, then ten, then fifty, until an entire section stood neat and cultivated. I measured progress not in hours but in acres, racing against the day's light, proud of each straight line carved into the earth. Out in the field, alone with the tractor and the sky, I felt a freedom I couldn't find anywhere else.

I wasn't old enough to drive legally, but in those hours I felt older than my years. The land stretched wide and endless, and for the first time, it belonged to me. Looking back, I see how those afternoons taught me more than farming—they taught me persistence, independence, and the quiet joy of working toward something bigger than myself.

Harvest was more than a season; it was a way of life. The dust, the sweat, the endless meals Mom prepared, and the quiet companionship of working side by side with Dad all carried lessons that stayed with me. Work until the job is done. Nothing is handed out freely. Perseverance comes from shared effort.

And yet, beneath those lessons was a deeper inheritance. My grandfather had left Norway at sixteen, unwilling to spend his life as a fisherman with little hope of prosperity. His courage carried him across the ocean, and his choice gave us the fields, the granary, and the pattern of harvest that defined my childhood.

I often imagined him standing at the edge of the sea, the salt wind in his hair, staring at a horizon that promised more than nets and waves. He traded the sound of gulls for the hum of binders, the roll of the tide for the roll of wagons heavy with grain. In every shock of wheat drying in the sun, in every wagon pulled by horses, in every meal spread across the farmhouse table, I saw the legacy of his decision.

He had exchanged water for soil, uncertainty for endurance, and in doing so, gave us a life built on fortitude and possibility, a foundation that carried us through toil, joy and the rhythms of farm life. And in those long August days, I learned that heritage is not just about where we come from, but about how we carry forward the strength of those who came before us.

When the last rows were cut and the fields finally exhaled, the farm settled into its quieter pulse. And as the weight of harvest lifted, a different kind of energy took its place—one measured not in bushels or hours, but in the laughter and footsteps of children eager to claim the open spaces as their own.

Adventures of Childhood

The fields taught us endurance, but the yard taught us joy. After the sweat of harvest and the pattern of chores, childhood found its own beat in games and adventures. Work shaped us, but play gave us balance, daring, and laughter. And nothing captured that balance more than the hammock stretched between the two old cottonwoods behind the farmhouse—the ones Dad said had been there longer than any of us.

Their bark was rough enough to scrape your palms if you slid your hand along it, and in summer it gave off a dusty, earthy smell that mixed with the scent of warm grass. At seven and nine, Gary and I had to take a running jump to scramble into the hammock, the ropes squeaking as if warning us to behave.

Once we settled, the hammock cupped us in its loose belly, swaying with that gentle, floating rhythm only farm kids knew—half breeze, half our own restless kicking. The woven cotton pressed patterns into the backs of our thighs, warm from the sun. When the wind stirred, it carried the smell of hay from the barn and the faint sweetness of alfalfa baking in the heat. Somewhere behind us, a cow mooed, a low bellowing sound, lazily, as if reminding us she still existed.

From the hammock, the sky seemed impossibly wide, a bright prairie blue that made you feel small in the best way. We'd watch the clouds drift over the fields, naming them:

"That one's a horse," Gary would say, pointing with a dusty toe. "No, it's a dragon," I'd insist, until the shape dissolved into something else entirely.

Sometimes the two of us would try to swing higher, kicking off the cottonwood trunk with bare feet—earning a shout from Mom if she spotted us. Other times we simply rocked back and forth, listening to the chickens fussing near the coop and the soft hum of insects swarming the tree or taking turns pushing each other as high as it could go. The whole farm seemed to exhale around us, slow and steady.

I remember the feel of the hammock tightening when Gary shifted his weight, and the sudden lurch that made us both grab the sides and laugh so hard our stomachs hurt. The sound carried across the yard, mingling with the wind in the corn and the creak of the clothesline poles.

Nothing flashy happened in that old hammock, but it held long summer afternoons when the world felt huge, safe, and ours. It was just the two of us—sunburnt, barefoot, swinging between the trees as if time had decided to pause for a while.

Trees were not only for hammocks. Two kinds of swings—a tire swing and one with a wooden platform—became our favorite playgrounds, long before electronics tried to compete for a child's attention. The tire swing hung from a thick, high limb deep in the woods near our farmhouse, a discarded rubber tire given new life with a sturdy rope. Dad had drilled holes in the bottom so rainwater wouldn't pool and invite clouds of mosquitos. My brother and I could sit inside the circle or balance on top, gripping the rope as we pushed off and sent ourselves soaring.

We spent hours taking turns: pushing each other higher, spinning until we were dizzy, or climbing in together to see how much weight the rope could hold. One of my favorite tricks was twisting the ropes tight while Gary sat inside the tire—then letting go and watching him spin wildly, laughing so hard he toppled into the grass afterward. Other times, I'd sit quietly in the gentle sway, watching clouds drift across the sky and letting the woods settle into silence around me.

Our second swing—a two-foot plank of scrap wood—hung from a tree by the shanty and offered a different kind of thrill. Gary and I pumped our legs furiously, shouting "Higher, higher!" as we tried to reach the lowest branches. When we wanted an extra challenge, we gave each other "underdogs"—running under the swing at just the right moment, careful not to be clipped by the returning arc, yelling "Underdoggggg!" as the swinger shot forward with new momentum.

Sometimes we turned it into a competition: I'd swing as high as courage allowed, then leap into the grass, calling, "Watch me!" to see who could land farthest. On hot summer days, the swings were more than toys—they were our cooling stations, lifting us into pockets of breeze beneath the shade of the old trees, offering a small, simple respite from the sun.

The yard offered endless inventions—when we weren't flying from swings, we were rolling inside tires. Adventures were simple, but no less exhilarating. We climbed into the hollow center of an old tractor tire and let gravity do the rest. The first few rolls were a dare: who could push the tire the farthest, who would laugh the loudest as it tipped and tumbled. Soon it became ritual. Green and brown streaked past in a dizzying blur, sunlight stabbing through the rim one instant and the dark rubber wrapping you the next. The tire's steady thump-thump-thump-thump—was like a drumbeat underscoring our screams and whoops. Gravel spat at the edge, and distant dogs barked like an audience cheering on our dangerous trick.

A sudden jolt sent us spilling from the tire into a soft ragged heap at the driveway's bottom. Breath blown out of us and grass in our hair, we lay staring up through the oak branches as leaves whispered. "That was huge!" Gary laughed, spitting dust. "You're going to push me next," I promised, already planning a higher start.

Not all our games carried the thrill of tumbling headlong down a hill. Some were quieter, but no less alive. On the driveway we drew crooked hopscotch squares in chalk, the stone clattering across the boxes as we hopped on one foot, wobbling, laughing when we tipped over. At dusk we played hide-and-seek, hearts pounding as shadows stretched across the yard. Gary's voice rang out, "Ready or not!" and the thrill was in the silence—waiting, holding breath, until discovery came with a shout.

Marbles clicked in the dirt, their glass swirls catching the sun in blues and greens. We crouched low, serious as gamblers, each strike a small victory. Jacks scattered across the kitchen floor, silver stars flashing as the ball bounced, our fingers darting quick and clumsy while laughter echoed off the walls. And when the rope slapped against the driveway in steady rhythm, we counted aloud, voices rising with each jump: "One, two, three..." The rhythm was ours, the challenge endless.

Some games we invented ourselves. Fence rails became balance beams, hay bales turned into castles, and sticks became swords in battles that stretched across the yard. We staged "farmyard Olympics," daring each other to climb higher, jump farther, or race faster. Even chores became play—chasing chickens, daring each other to sneak past the geese, or turning the pump handle into a contest of strength.

Of all our daring games, none was more outrageous than the day Gary decided a calf would make a fine substitute for a pony. My brother was always looking for adventure, and before we had Pepper, our pony, riding a calf seemed second best. Hunched over the calf, arms flailing for balance, his face showed a mix of determination and a little fear. The calf tried to run, ears pinned back and tail swishing, its body twisting in short, jerky bursts as it bucked to dislodge him. Dust and grass flew up from its hooves, and I watched in disbelief as it snorted and bellowed, "MOOOO! MOOOO!" Gary laughed hysterically, the thud of his feet against the calf's sides echoing with each stride. Mom, hearing the commotion, came running out of the house shouting, "Get off, before you get hurt." Sheepishly, Gary slid off, looped a rope around its neck, and led it back to the barnyard from where it had escaped.

Gary's calf-riding stunt was only one of the many ways we tested our courage on the farm. When the animals weren't our playground, the trees were—beckoning us upward into worlds of imagination and daring.

Climbing trees in the 1940s carried another kind of magic that's hard to recapture today. Back then, trees weren't just trees—to Gary and I, they were lookout towers, pirate ships, secret forts, and escape routes. All the farm kids treated them like natural playgrounds, their branches a challenge and an invitation. With fewer distractions and a whole lot more freedom to roam, we turned to the world outside as our entertainment, and the tallest oak or maple was often the crown jewel of the forest behind our house.

Gary and I knew every good climbing tree within the perimeters of our farm—where the bark was rough but steady, which branches formed the perfect staircase upward, and how high we dared to go without an adult noticing. Climbing was an adventure fueled by imagination, bravery, and just a touch of mischief.

And into that world of barefoot scrapes and skinned knees came the day a tall maple "captured" Gary's attention. He must have thought he'd found the perfect hideaway—a spot way up where he felt untouchable, commander of the treetops. But there he was: perched on a sturdy branch, pants hanging from another limb like a flag of surrender, completely preoccupied with the very serious business of peeing from on high.

My mom, had a friend visiting. As they approached the farmhouse, they followed the giggles and a mysterious dripping sound, only to look up and catch him mid-act. A tiny king of the tree, trousers waving overhead, absolutely pleased with himself. Mom hollered up at him, half shocked, half laughing, "Get down before you fall down."

It became one of those stories—retold for years, always funnier with each retelling—rooted in a time when childhood was lived outside, adventures were self-made, and even a tree could turn into a stage for unforgettable mischief. That wasn't the only mischief!

Gary was always chasing experiences bigger than his age. One afternoon he decided that adulthood meant smoking, and since cigarettes were off-limits, he improvised. I found him crouched behind the couch like a pint-sized outlaw, Mom's precious end papers, those thin, porous white sheets from her home permanent kit, rolled tight between his fingers. Mom would twist those papers around the ends of her hair before winding it onto a rod; the paper protected the hair from the harsh chemicals used in the perming process.

He'd stuffed them with damp coffee grounds scooped straight from the tin, and the moment he saw me he struck a match. I watched him light it with shaking hands and a determined little jaw, wanting so badly to feel older, tougher.

There he was: eyes watering, trying to puff on a soggy "cigarette" that smelled like burnt dirt and impending doom. A thin curl of smoke rose like a confession. Gary coughed, choked, and then grinned at me with black coffee flecks stuck to his teeth. Any hope of hiding the evidence vanished with the acrid smell that drifted straight toward Mom in the kitchen.

Frantically, entering the living room, shocked, she exclaimed, "Here you are trying to set your lungs and the house on fire! Take a timeout in the corner and we'll talk about it."

But the farm wasn't the only place for fun and games; our social circle was a world unto itself. Community added its own flavor. At church socials, friends joined in, their laughter mixing with ours until the games felt endless. Rivalries sparked, victories were celebrated, and defeats forgotten in the glow of lanterns and the promise of pie cooling on the table.

At school recess, we played softball with scuffed bats and balls that barely held their stitching. Dodgeball was a popular, brutal game, where I didn't want to be the last one chosen on the team, nor hit in the head by the rubber ball. The rule was hit below the waist, but with the excitement of the game, anything could happen. Playing tag with boys chasing the girls was a common game with shouts of "You're it!" and the sounds of running feet on the school playground. "Ha! Ha! You didn't catch me!" I'd tease at the top of my lungs.

Looking back, those games and adventures were more than ways to pass time. They taught us balance, patience, timing, and the thrill of risk. They stitched childhood into the fabric of our days, laughter echoing across fields and driveways, teaching us lessons disguised as play. In the tire's tumble we learned daring; in hopscotch, persistence; in marbles, the beauty of small victories; in jump rope, endurance. Together they formed the cadence of our childhood, a pattern that would echo long after the games and adventures were gone.

Blankets of White and Wonder

And just as those summer games shaped us, winter offered its own kind of daring. Outside the walls of school, snow transformed the world into a bright, breathy playground. The fields that had been golden with grain now lay hushed and white, the fences softened, the barns capped with frosted roofs. Gary and I hurled ourselves down the hill on a dented runner sled, the wind punching our cheeks until we howled with glee. The sled rattled over frozen ruts, sparks of ice spraying at the edges, and we clung to each other, half-terrified, half-ecstatic, until the world blurred into speed.

We built forts with tunneled entrances and stacked banks, crouching inside like tiny commanders while snowballs thudded against the walls. The battles were fierce but short-lived, ending in laughter when gloves grew too stiff to throw. Making snow angels became a race to leave the prettiest wings; we flattened our backs, swept our arms wide, and scrambled up to compare prints, the sky above us a pale dome that seemed to bless our efforts.

Fox and geese carved a map into the field—tracks for foxes to hunt and geese to guard—and the game could last until dusk, our feet numb and laughter puffing out like tiny clouds. Sometimes we chased each other across the frozen yard, our boots squeaking against packed snow, until the cold bit so hard it felt like our faces might crack.

Coming inside was its own ritual. Mittens peeled off, boots stomped clean, scarves unwound in a heap by the door. The farmhouse smelled of wood smoke and bread, and we cradled steaming mugs of hot chocolate made with whole milk, a splash of vanilla, and a fat spoonful of whipped cream. "One more sip," Gary begged, fingers pink and trembling. "No, you'll drip on the quilt," I'd reply, but I slid the cup across anyway. The warmth tasted like victory, a sweet reward for braving the cold.

Those winter games were more than diversions; they were rehearsals for endurance. The sting of wind on our cheeks, the ache of numb feet, the thrill of pushing past discomfort—all of it taught us how to meet the world head-on. Childhood was measured in seasons, each one shaping us differently: summer gave us fields to roam, autumn gave us harvest, and winter gave us endurance and resolve.

As the snow melted and the fields reappeared, play gave way to responsibility. The same hills we sledded down became the backdrop for chores, lessons, and the slow march toward growing up. School days stretched longer, farm work demanded more, and I began to sense that childhood's games were giving way to something larger—tasks that carried weight, choices that carried consequence.

But winter wasn't only sleds and snowball fights. It was also the season of holidays, when play gave way to ritual and the farmhouse filled with the smells of tradition. The kitchen glowed with kerosene light, pies cooling on the counter, and the sharp scent of pine drifted from the tree Dad had cut from the grove. Voices gathered around the piano, carols rising against the hush of snow outside. Packages wrapped in brown paper and tied with twine sat beneath the tree, their promise as bright as the ornaments that caught the lamplight.

In those moments, winter felt less like endurance and more like celebration. The cold pressed against the windows, but inside there was warmth—of food, of family, of traditions that bound us together.

Feasts, Faith, and Christmas Eve Magic

The holidays in the 1950's were more than celebrations; they were lessons in tradition, faith, and family. At Grandma's house, Thanksgiving and Christmas meant learning the old ways—lefse, krumkake, rømmegrøt, and even lutefisk—dishes that carried Norway into our Minnesota farmhouse kitchen. The kitchen filled with the smell of butter sizzling on the griddle, flour dust rising like snow as Grandma rolled lefse thin enough to see light through. She moved with a rhythm born of repetition, her hands sure, her voice humming a hymn under her breath.

Coats piled high on the bed, cousins tumbled through the hallways, and the grown-ups spoke in Norwegian, their voices clipped and musical. Candlelight flickered against frosted windows, and the table groaned under platters of food. We bowed our heads as Grandpa prayed, his words steady, reminding us that gratitude was more than a holiday—it was a way of life.

After supper, we gathered around the piano, voices rising in carols, the lamplight catching the shine of ornaments on the tree. Gifts were simple—hand-knit mittens, jars of preserves, sometimes an orange tucked into a stocking—but they carried the weight of love. Looking back, I see how those holidays stitched together more than family; they stitched together identity. Each dish, each hymn, each candle was a thread tying us to a heritage that shaped who we were and who we would become.

Lefse was always the centerpiece. Grandma began with riced potatoes, butter, and cream, mixing them into a soft dough that chilled overnight. In the morning, after adding flour, she rolled the dough into balls and flattened them on a floured table. The rolling pin clattered rhythmically—whack, whack, whack—as the dough stretched thinner and thinner, almost translucent. Each round was lifted with a slender wooden "lefse stick" and laid across the hot stovetop. In less than a minute, brown freckles appeared, marking it ready. Later, when electricity came, she proudly used her new electric lefse grill, but the ritual remained the same. Warm lefse was served with butter and sugar, rolled into sweet treats, or alongside hearty meals like beef stew.

Krumkake was another delight, fragile and festive. Grandma poured a spoonful of batter—flour, sugar, eggs, butter, and cardamom—onto the heavy iron resting on her stovetop. In seconds, the batter browned, releasing a sweet, spiced aroma. She quickly lifted it off and rolled it around a cone-shaped mold, her hands moving with practiced speed before the cookie cooled. Once crisp, the cookies were tucked into tins, waiting for whipped cream and berries to fill their hollow centers. To me, they were little treasures of Christmas, delicate and joyful.

Rømmegrøt carried with it not only flavor but folklore. Grandma told me how, in Norway, families left a bowl of the creamy porridge out on Christmas Eve for the *nisse*—the red-capped house elf—to ensure good fortune for the farm.

Made from sour cream, milk, and flour, rømmegrøt was thick and rich, served warm with melted butter and a dusting of cinnamon and sugar. Though sweet, it was never considered dessert; it was a dish of celebration, often paired with lutefisk at Christmastime.

Ah, lutefisk! That peculiar dish of dried cod, soaked in lye until it turned gelatinous, then rinsed for days in cold water. Its texture was slippery, its flavor mild but unmistakably alkaline. Some loved it, others turned up their noses. Grandma served it with boiled potatoes, green peas, and bacon, insisting it was a taste of heritage. For me, lutefisk was less about the flavor and more about the ritual—the way it brought family together, laughter around the table, and stories of Norway that reminded us who we were.

And then came Christmas Eve. Grandma's house glowed with warmth, the tree standing tall in the corner, its branches heavy with ornaments and presents tucked beneath. The scent of pine mingled with the aroma of holiday dishes, and the hum of voices filled every room. Before gifts were opened, Grandma gathered us together and read the Christmas story. Her voice was gentle but firm, carrying the words of scripture with reverence. As children, we squirmed with anticipation, eyes darting toward the packages under the tree, but we knew the story came first. It was her way of reminding us that Christmas was more than ribbons and paper—it was faith, family, and tradition.

Often, after the story, we bundled into coats and scarves and walked to the candlelight service at the little church on the corner. That church was more than a building; it was where we attended Sunday School during the school year, where hymns echoed against wooden pews, and where community meant everything. On Christmas Eve, the sanctuary glowed with candlelight, each flame flickering in unison as voices rose in carols. I remember the hush that fell when "Silent Night" began, the candles held high, the soft harmony wrapping around us like a blanket.

Those evenings were magical. The gifts under the tree were exciting, of course, but what lingers in memory is the feeling of belonging—the warmth of Grandma's voice, the glow of candles, the closeness of family. The food, the faith, the laughter—all of it wove together into a tapestry of heritage and love. Christmas was not just a holiday; it was a ritual of identity, a reminder that even in the coldest Minnesota winters, light and joy could fill a home.

As I look back on those holiday gatherings—the lefse sizzling on Grandma's stove, the krumkake crisping in its iron, the rømmegrøt thick and comforting, and the candlelight service that filled the church with song—I see more than food and ritual. I see the legacy of my grandfather, who left Norway at sixteen, unwilling to spend his life as a fisherman with little hope of prosperity. He carried with him not only courage but culture, and it was in our kitchens and churches that his heritage lived on.

The traditions my grandmother kept alive were more than recipes or routines; they were acts of remembrance, a way of honoring the journey that brought our family to Minnesota. Each bite of lefse, each hymn sung by candlelight, was a thread connecting us to the past, reminding us that survival and faith were as much a part of our inheritance as the language and customs of Norway.

Grandpa's choice to leave the sea shaped the life I was born into—a life where farming, family, and faith defined our days. And though I never stood on the deck of a fishing boat in Norway, I carried his story with me every Christmas Eve, knowing that the warmth of our gatherings was built on his sacrifice. In the glow of Grandma's tree and the taste of her lefse, I understood that heritage is not just about where we come from, but about how we choose to keep it alive.

And as the candles of Christmas faded and winter slowly loosened its grip, our lives turned outward again. The thaw carried us from Grandma's kitchen to the yard, where the first warm days called us upward into the branches of the giant oak. Childhood's cadence shifted with the seasons—faith and family indoors, freedom and invention outdoors.

Smoke Rising From the Treehouse

As winter loosened its grip and the snow melted into rivulets that trickled through the yard, our world shifted upward. The giant oak at the edge of the farm became our kingdom, its branches stretching wide like arms ready to hold us. With hammer, nails, and scavenged boards, we built a treehouse that was less a structure than a dream balanced among limbs.

The climb itself was part of the ritual. The bark scraped our hands, the boards creaked under our weight, and each rung of the ladder felt like a step into another realm. From the ground, it looked precarious, but once inside, the treehouse felt eternal—solid, secret, and ours alone.

Inside, sunlight filtered through cracks in the boards, striping the floor with golden lines. We furnished it with whatever we could carry: old crates for chairs, a tin box for treasures, a blanket draped across one corner for shade. The air smelled of sap and sawdust, and the wind whispered through the leaves, making the walls hum with life.

From that perch, the farm looked different. The barn roof gleamed in the distance, the fields stretched like a patchwork quilt, and the yard below seemed smaller, safer. We spied on the world from above, inventing stories about travelers crossing the gravel road or imagining ourselves as explorers charting new lands.

The treehouse became more than a play space—it was a sanctuary. We whispered secrets there, plotted adventures, and sometimes just sat in silence, listening to the steady heartbeat of the farm below. It was the first place that felt truly ours, built not by parents or grandparents but by our own hands, woven with together with imagination and nails.

We built the treehouse high in the giant oak north of the yard—a crooked floor of gray planks, a railing sanded by our small, stubborn hands, and a doorway that smelled of sap and summer. Sunlight drew patterns across the boards by day; at night, fireflies formed a slow constellation just outside the slats. From that perch, the world felt larger, and so did we.

The tree house had its rules. "No dropping mud pies from the railing," Dad warned the first time he climbed up to inspect our handiwork. Gary grinned, lifting a lopsided pie. "Promise," he said, though his eyes already gleamed with mischief. I crossed my arms. "Don't make me tell."

We kept a quilt my grandma had stitched folded in a corner; it smelled faintly of lavender and flour. Knees tucked beneath our chins, we traded stories until the air cooled. "Do you think there are pirates in that swamp?" Gary would whisper, pointing toward the low, misty slough. "Only if they can row on ice," I'd counter, but the shadow of possibility made our voices softer.

One evening, our ordinary play bent toward the extraordinary. We'd been whittling small whistles when a distant shout cut through the trees. "Donna! Gary! Time to come in!" Mom's voice carried, tight with worry. We froze, then scrambled down the ladder, scraping our palms on the bark. At the bottom, Mom's face was flushed; Dad held a lantern and a blanket. "There's a storm coming faster than I thought," he said. "We all need to get inside, now." Gary clutched my hand. "We forgot the little whistle," he hissed, glancing at the dark outline of the tree. I squeezed back. "It'll wait. We'll get it tomorrow." That night, the tree house felt less like an escape and more like a lookout that had taught us when to come home.

Our afternoons often blurred into experiments of mischief. We loved making mud pies—mixing the silken, sun-baked dirt with water from the old rain barrel until it turned into something that could be shaped and "baked." That afternoon the game tipped toward danger.

"Look what I found," Gary said, hefting a half-buried, rusty metal container behind the barn. He set it down and grinned like every secret was a promise. I ducked into the chicken coop fetching our "secret ingredient." The air inside was warm and sour, full of feathers and the sharp tang of ammonia. I returned with two still-warm, brown-speckled eggs, the straw clinging to their shells tickling my palm and followed him to the tree house clearing.

Gary tapped the first one on the stump's edge, letting the contents—a thick, orange yolk and clear runny slop directly into our thick, chocolatey mixture. I cracked the second one, the yolk breaking and swirling like liquid gold. into the mix. Our fingers blending the water, dirt and secret ingredients like a magical blender, making the mud feel smooth and pliable as baker's dough. We patted and molded our pies on a flat stump, proud architects of mud, our hands caked in the earthy batter.

Then Gary's eyes landed on the red gas tank by the granary. He rummaged and came back with an old tin can, fingers stained with oil. "This'll make them bake faster," he said, voice low as if inventing mischief was a sacred duty.

He poured. The smell of gasoline cut the summer air—bright, chemical, oddly familiar. Gary struck a match. The tiny flare lit his face for a heartbeat. "Don't—" I started, then the match hit the can's fumes. A whoosh exploded upward, heat hitting our hands like a sudden, incredulous slap. The mud pies ignited in a quick, greedy flash.

For a second the world narrowed to sound: the hiss of flame, the crack of dry grass, our own breathing. We tumbled for the rain barrel, flinging water, then quickly, scooping and throwing dirt until the fire spat and died in a gray, smoking heap. The farmhouse glowed in the distance as if the barn had caught fire and we had not yet realized the scale of what might have been.

We stood panting, hands caked in mud and ash, the mud pies still warm from the heat. Gary's eyes were wide and blinking. "We—" He couldn't finish. I felt a small, fierce relief that bordered on shame.

Mom never knew that night. We rubbed our hands raw and swept the ashes away like guilty footprints. For a long time, the brush with disaster lived as a secret, a story we'd later tell with nervous laughter about how fast a dare can turn into something that eats the world around you.

The fire taught us how quickly play could tip into danger,

how a spark could threaten the world we thought was ours to command. Yet even with the sting of smoke still in our memory, we kept chasing the edge of adventure.

But as spring ripened into summer, the treehouse became only the beginning. The long evenings stretched like promises, and we carried our games outward into the fields and the slough. Barefoot, we raced through tall grass, the blades slapping against our legs, cicadas buzzing like a chorus above. Fireflies blinked in the dusk, tiny lanterns we chased with jars, their glow flickering against our palms before we let them go.

The slough was another kingdom. We dammed the edges with rocks, daring the water to rise, and splashed until our clothes clung heavy and wet. Minnows darted between our toes, and frogs leapt from the banks, their croaks echoing like laughter. We built rafts from scrap boards, testing them against the current, shouting triumph when they floated, groaning when they sank.

Summer nights carried their own magic. We lay on our backs in the grass, staring at constellations, inventing names for stars we didn't know. The air smelled of clover and alfalfa, and the horizon glowed faintly with lightning bugs and distant storms. In those moments, the farm felt endless, the world wide open, and childhood infinite.

The treehouse had given us a perch to dream from, but summer gave us the ground to run on, the water to splash in, and the sky to wonder at. Together, they blended freedom into our days, preparing us for the next adventure—the pony that would carry us farther still, into fields and pastures we had only imagined from the oak's high branches and test our courage in a different way.

The Ride of My Life

Dad traded the work horses for a pony, and in that moment the farm shifted. The big draft horses had been the muscle of our fields, their broad backs pulling plows and wagons, their steady pace marking the rhythm of labor. When they left, the yard felt strangely empty, as though a chapter of our farm's strength had closed. In their place stood Pepper—a black-and-brown speckled pony, small but wiry, with eyes that seemed to measure us as much as we measured him.

Gary and I circled him like new recruits sizing up a commander. His mane was coarse, his tail flicked with impatience, and his ears twitched at every sound. He was no plow horse, no steady worker; he was built for mischief and speed. We named him Pepper, a name that fit his restless energy, his quick steps, his sharp gaze.

Gary, always the teacher and trickster, took charge. He taught Pepper every signal—halt, lead, pace—but kept the cues to himself, a secret language between boy and pony. So when I swung into the saddle, I was blindsided, finding myself in a game where Gary held all the cards

I tightened the cinch, the coarse hair under my palms prickling. "Remember, don't pull the reins," Gary called, smirking from the fence. "Just sit still." I nodded, boots digging into the stirrups. No helmet, of course. The farm smelled of hay and manure and something sharper under

Pepper's nose that made the air feel taut. The air itself seemed to hold its breath.

At first Pepper walked polite and slow, the cadence of hooves like a steady drum. I sat tall, almost proud, imagining myself a real rider—someone in control, someone who knew what she was doing. Then the gait changed: a skittish shuffle, a quickening that sent a thin thread of worry through my chest as the world began to slide sideways through the trees. My stomach tightened. I grabbed for the horn of the saddle just as the pony lengthened into a full gallop. Wind slapped my face; my breath came sharp and shallow. "Easy, Pepper—easy!" I yelled, though my voice cracked with more hope than authority. Gary's laugh floated back toward me: "You look like a rodeo star!"—and then even that vanished into the rush of air and pounding hooves.

Without warning Pepper reared, front legs cleaving the sky. The air left me in a sharp, cold gasp; the world narrowed to the dark rim of the saddle and the hard taste of fear. Then Pepper dropped back to all fours and bolted toward the barn with a frantic, thundering rush. I slid from the saddle with shaking legs, hands smelling of hay and adrenaline. Gary met me at the gate, eyes wide now and no grin. "You okay?" he asked. I laughed shakily. "Never again," I said—meaning it, and not meaning it at all.

Later, I realized Pepper had taught me something the treehouse never could: that daring wasn't only about imagination, it was about trust—trust in the animal beneath me, trust in my own balance, trust in knowing when to hold on and when to let go. The silence of the era meant no one explained these lessons outright, but the pony carried them into me all the same. In Pepper's wild rush I felt both fear and freedom, a combination that marked the beginning of my becoming.

But not all lessons arrived with the thunder of hooves or the thrill of speed. Some came quietly, without warning, slipping past the fences and fields into the stillness of an ordinary afternoon. Only later did I understand that Pepper had been preparing me—teaching me to trust my balance so I'd be ready when the world tilted in ways that had nothing to do with galloping hooves.

The same year I tested my bravery on Pepper's back, I faced a different kind of trial—one that no amount of daring could outrun. It came not with adrenaline but with silence, not with exhilaration but with grief. That year, I lost my cat, and the lesson was no longer about holding on—it was about letting go.

Tiny Coffin Beneath the Apple Tree

The first sound shredded the afternoon: a sharp slam of the porch door, like a hand striking wood. On the sun-warmed porch, we found our Siamese, still as if asleep. At first, I thought she was merely resting; the curve of her body was familiar, the tilt of her head unchanged. But the stillness resolved into something final, a silence too complete to mistake.

Our hands—so used to the warmth and velvet of her fur—felt only cold. The towel she favored held the ghost of her scent, making the loss tactile and unbearably near. I pressed my face into it, hoping for one more trace of her, but even that comfort was fading.

We wrapped her like a promise and carried her toward the trees, each step too loud, ordinary noises insisting the world had not stopped for us. The hollow beneath the pines felt like the right size for what we were doing. The soil was cool and smelled of rain as we lowered her gently, covering her with earth. Birds called as if nothing had changed; their bright notes felt like unfair punctuation. I whispered, "She liked this spot," and Gary nodded, motion small and solemn.

We lingered longer than we needed to, brushing dirt from our hands, listening to the woods breathe around us. The air seemed heavier, as if it knew what we had done. Walking home, we expected the familiar brush against our legs, the jingle of a tiny collar, the soft weight curling at our feet. When none of that came, the absence made the world too loud.

The Siamese had been more than a pet; she was a companion woven into the fabric of our days. She greeted us at the door, curled into our laps, and claimed the porch as her throne. Her absence was not just the loss of an animal—it was the loss of a pulse, a presence that had made the farm feel more alive.

I remember Gary trying to make me laugh, tossing a pinecone into the air, saying, "She'd chase this if she were here." But the joke fell flat, and we both knew it. Grief had a way of silencing even our games.

That day was the first time I understood that love could leave a silence behind. It was not the kind of danger we had learned to outrun, but a different kind of trial—one that taught us how fragile joy could be, and how memory sometimes has to stand in for presence. In the hush of the pines, I began to realize that growing up meant carrying both laughter and loss, stitched together in ways we could not yet name.

But grief was not the only shadow that year. Loss had shown us how quickly the world could change, yet another trial waited—this time inside my own body. Where the cat's stillness had taught me absence, illness would teach me how thin the line was between presence and disappearance.

It began quietly, with a cough, no more alarming than a tickle in the throat. But soon it grew into something larger, a storm no game or dare could prepare me for. The lessons of Pepper's wild rush and the silence beneath the pines had been about courage and loss. Now, I would learn about vulnerability—the kind that comes when your own body betrays you.

The Fight for Air

It began with a cough that rattled my chest, then a fever that burned hotter than any summer sun. I remember the weight of blankets pressing down, the air thick and hard to swallow, my body shrinking against the enormity of illness. Outside, the farm carried on—chores done, animals fed, the pattern of life unbroken—but inside, I lay suspended between breath and silence. For the first time, I felt how fragile even the strongest roots could be, and how survival itself could feel like a borrowed gift.

I woke one morning when I was about eleven years old with a terror I had never known before: I could not breathe. My chest felt locked, as though invisible hands were squeezing the air out of me. Each gasp was shallow, each attempt at breath a desperate struggle. Mom, frantic, called the clinic in Fergus Falls, twenty miles from our farm. I still remember the tremor in her voice as she pleaded for an appointment. The answer was cold and routine: no openings. The advice was to give me hot chicken soup and let me rest. They had no idea how close I was to slipping away.

By afternoon, my breathing had worsened. I wheezed with a high-pitched whistle, like a kettle shrieking on the stove, and every inhale rattled with bubbling crackles deep in my chest. My lips turned a frightening shade of blue. Mom's eyes widened in panic, and Dad's jaw tightened with resolve. Without hesitation, they bundled me into the truck, gravel spitting behind us as we sped toward Pelican Rapids. Fergus Falls had failed us; Pelican Rapids was our only hope.

At the health center, doctors rushed to stabilize me. A T-shaped nasotracheal tube was slid through my nose, forcing air into my lungs. The sting of the tube was sharp, but the rush of oxygen was a relief so profound I thought I might cry. My treatment shifted to antibiotics, penicillin among them, delivered through disposable syringes. For many, penicillin was a miracle. For me, it was nothing but a waiting game. My body did not respond.

Weeks stretched on in the hospital. The sterile white walls became my world, but children are resourceful, even in sickness. We scavenged syringes from wastebaskets, filled them with water, and gave our pillows and mattresses "shots." Soon, the ward erupted into syringe gun battles. "Got you!" I shouted, spraying water across the face of a girl from a nearby town who was also fighting pneumonia. Our laughter echoed down the hallways, defying the illness that kept us there. In those moments, we were not patients but children reclaiming joy.

Still, recovery was slow. Doctors struggled to identify the culprit behind my pneumonia. Penicillin failed, suggesting either a viral infection or a resistant bacterial strain. In the 1950s, medicine often meant managing symptoms and hoping the body could endure. Eventually, I was discharged into the care of my grandmother, who believed in remedies passed down through generations.

Grandma's mustard plaster was her weapon against my cough. She mixed ground mustard with flour and water, spread the paste on a cloth, and pressed it against my chest. The burn was immediate, my skin reddening beneath the heat. She applied it daily, convinced it would draw out the sickness. I lay there, chest stinging, listening to her hum old hymns as she worked. Her faith in the plaster was unshakable, and though I doubted its power, I never doubted hers. In her hands, healing was as much love as medicine.

My hacking cough was relentless, a rattling reminder of how close I'd come to the edge. The turning point arrived with a small, mysterious medicine bottle. The doctor prescribed a single, potent "drop" to be mixed into a glass of water, and its effect was nothing short of miraculous. The concoction, likely containing ingredients common in 1950s remedies such as ephedrine or pseudoephedrine, cut through the congestion and offered immense relief.

In that era, cough medicines often included powerful, now-regulated substances like codeine, morphine, or even chloroform, all designed to suppress coughs and induce sleep. The "miraculous drop" was effective, whether due to these strong ingredients or simply my immune system finally overcoming the infection, aided by Grandma's supportive care.

I survived that close call and eventually returned to school. Yet, the ordeal left a lasting mark. The recurring bouts of pneumonia that followed signaled a weakened immune system, a vulnerability that makes fighting off infections challenging to this day. The experience ties into a somber historical reality: a peak in pneumonia mortality rates in 1957 was caused by the severe Asian influenza (H2N2) pandemic, which disproportionately affected school children and young adults. The pandemic highlighted how secondary bacterial infections, like pneumonia, became particularly deadly during widespread viral outbreaks.

Twice I had felt how thin the line was between breath and silence, and twice I had returned. Childhood was no longer only forts and ponies, cats and laughter—it carried shadows now, reminders that life could be fragile, unfair, and demanding. Those shadows would follow me into adolescence, shaping the awakenings that were waiting for me.

PART II: SHADOWS AND AWAKENINGS

"In the middle of difficulty lies opportunity."
— **Albert Einstein**

Growing older meant stepping beyond the fields into classrooms, dances, and struggles that tested identity. Shadows of discrimination and illness mingled with awakenings of love, rebellion, and the first stirrings of independence.

Sanctuary and Stage

Worship was the center of our week. On Sundays, the farm seemed to pause, its rhythms bending toward the church bell that tolled across fields and gravel roads. The morning began with ritual: shoes polished until they shone, dresses pressed, white stockings, hair brushed smooth, the smell of starch and soap filling the kitchen. The drive down gravel roads felt ceremonial, neighbors waving as they walked, the bell's echo pulling us all toward the same place.

Inside the sanctuary, sunlight fractured through stained glass, scattering color across the pews. Hymnals creaked open, voices rose imperfect but joined, and the wooden floor groaned under the shuffle of shoes. Faith was not only in the words spoken but in the cadence of sound—the organ's hum, the rustle of pages, the collective exhale of prayer.

Dad served as a deacon for years until illness forced him to step down; Mom belonged to Ladies Aid and hosted Circle Bible Study in living rooms that smelled of coffee and cinnamon. The church wasn't just a place to pray—it was where life outside the farm folded into town: potlucks heavy with casseroles, basket socials where laughter carried across the fellowship hall, craft sales with tables lined in quilts and jams, and the long, neighborly conversations that followed the service. Faith was woven into food, fellowship, and the cadence of hymns.

Confirmation felt like stepping onto a stage. We stood

in white robes at the front of the sanctuary, the organ humming behind us, while the pastor asked us to recite answers we had learned by heart. My throat tightened as I said the words; my hands trembled on my lap. When the pastor asked, "Do you believe...?" a tiny voice inside me answered for both fear and faith. Afterward, the relief was almost as loud as the organ — a quiet, proud hush from the pews, a collective exhale of parents and grandparents who had waited for this moment.

A small memory always surfaces: the close, warm hand of my mother in the pew next to me, squeezing once when I forgot a line and squeezing again when I remembered it. That single touch steadied me more than any lesson ever could. In that squeeze was reassurance, pride, and a reminder that faith was not only doctrine but presence—someone beside you when you faltered.

Looking back, I see how worship shaped not only our weeks but our understanding of belonging. The church was a stage where we performed certainty, even when doubt lingered quietly inside. It was a place where questions were answered with memorized responses, where silence filled the gaps between what was spoken and what was felt. Faith gave me structure, but it also taught me how silence could live alongside devotion.

The church gave me a place to belong, a pulse that carried us from Sunday to Sunday. Yet even as faith offered structure and community, silence lingered in other corners of life—silence about bodies, about womanhood, about things too private to name. My next awakening came not in the sanctuary, but in the shadows of our own home.

Silence and Shadows

The only sex education available to me as a girl was a small, discreet book tucked on the bottom shelf of the end table beside the sofa—the kind of book that lived in shadows and whispered rather than spoke. Its pages were thin, its language clinical, and its presence almost secret. I never saw anyone open it, and I was too timid to ask. In our house, bodies were not discussed; they were managed quietly, as if acknowledging them too openly might invite shame.

So when I was mowing the lawn one summer afternoon and felt a sudden, stabbing pain low in my belly, the world seemed to tilt. In the bathroom, I watched the water swirl pink after I urinated. My chest tightened like a closing fist. The crimson stain on my underpants wasn't just a surprise—it was a shock that made my whole body feel foreign. With no words for what was happening, I leapt to terrifying conclusions: that I was gravely ill, that something inside me had ruptured, that I might be dying.

"Mom, come here—please. I'm not well," I whimpered.

She was beside me almost immediately—steady, calm, and unexpectedly gentle. Guiding me to sit on the closed toilet lid, she took my hand and explained, in a quiet, halting voice, what a period was, what I could expect, and how to take care of myself. Her words were simple and practical, but they unraveled my fear thread by thread.

"I thought I was dying," I whispered.

"You're not," she said. "This is part of being a woman. You'll learn how to manage it."

Her reassurance felt like a small rescue. At the same time, a flicker of anger sparked inside me—not anger at her, but at the silence that had left both of us unprepared. I carried that memory with me: the shock, the relief, and the quiet resolve that someday, if I could help it, no girl would feel that lost about her own body.

In the post-World War II 1940s and into the 1950s, American culture emphasized traditional gender roles, privacy, and a strict moral code. Topics like sex and menstruation were rarely discussed openly—not in schools, not in church, and often not even in families. My parents, shaped by both American norms and the Norwegian heritage woven through our Minnesota community, had grown up in an atmosphere of even greater reticence. Silence was considered modesty, and modesty was considered virtue.

Affection was private, too. I rarely saw my parents hug or kiss, or speak openly about their love for each other. As a child, I often felt I should be seen and not heard, absorbing the unspoken lesson that emotions—and bodies—were best kept under wraps. That silence shaped me as much as the hymns in the sanctuary. It taught me that becoming a woman meant learning to navigate what was hidden, to find resilience in what was never spoken aloud.

Looking back, I see that moment in the bathroom as my first true awakening. It was not just the beginning of menstruation—it was the beginning of awareness: of secrecy, of cultural expectations, of the gap between what was lived and what was said. In the hush of that afternoon, I stepped into shadows that would follow me into adolescence, shaping how I understood myself and the world around me.

The silence around bodies became a silence around identity. It taught me to carry questions quietly, to measure myself against standards I did not choose, and to find the strength to keep going in the spaces where words failed.

But silence did not stop at the bathroom door. It reached into classrooms, workplaces, and the wider world, where being a girl meant being underestimated, overlooked, or dismissed. If menstruation had taught me how unspoken truths could shape a life, discrimination taught me how spoken words could wound just as deeply.

My next awakening came not from the body, but from the way society measured it.

Lessons Beyond the Blackboard

In school, I began to notice the lines drawn between boys and girls—lines that determined who was called on, who was praised, and who was expected to lead. The lessons were not written in textbooks but in the pauses of teachers, the smirks of classmates, the subtle ways opportunity bent away from me. Discrimination was not always loud; often it was quiet, like a door closing softly before you could step through.

Our 1st–12th grade school felt like the town's heart. My brother and I walked a mile to the yellow bus that huffed up the hill; I'd shout, "Gary, hustle!" and we'd sprint the last stretch, backpacks thumping against our shoulders. Inside, the coatroom hooks and cubbies held the winter smell of wool coats and rubber boots close to our desks. Mittens and gloves dangled from long strings threaded through sleeves so they wouldn't be lost. The classrooms smelled faintly of chalk dust and floor polish, the blackboards streaked with half-erased lessons. At recess, the town girls skipped rope in perfect rhythm while we farm kids played tag in boots that left clumsy tracks in the snow. I ate lunch at school—hamburger gravy on mashed potatoes was my favorite, the steam rising from the tray like comfort itself.

Second grade brought the twins, Daryl and Dayle, from Minneapolis, and they turned our class of twenty-two into a spectacle. My cousin, Marlyce, and I spent special times reading with them in the narrow coatroom; years later, Daryl and I married, and Dayle married my cousin—tiny thickets of connection that grew into a life. Even then, I felt the school was more than lessons; it was a place where futures quietly took root.

My memories of third and fourth grade are very different. Most of those years are a blur, except for one moment that stands out. My aunt, who was my teacher then, stood at the blackboard, chalk in hand, writing. I sat in a wooden desk with a hinged lift-up top, an inkwell, and a groove for pencils, the rows of desks lined neatly before her. As I reread what she had written, I noticed a spelling mistake. Wanting to help, I quietly walked up to her and pointed it out. Instead of thanking me, she swatted me on the backside and sent me back to my seat. That moment stayed with me—not because of the sting, but because it taught me how easily a child's eagerness can be discouraged.

By contrast, my fifth-grade teacher showed me what it meant to awaken possibility. She saw something in me that I didn't yet see in myself, and through small acts of encouragement—like handing me extra worksheets to explore at home—she nourished my curiosity and gave me the confidence to dream of becoming a teacher.

The best classroom teachers are the ones who believe, as Helen Keller once said, that "every child has hidden away within them noble capacities waiting to be brought out if only we know how to go about doing it."

My teacher believed in those hidden capacities. She

understood that education was not only about arithmetic and spelling, but about awakening a sense of possibility in each child. Robert Frost captured this truth when he wrote, "I am not a teacher but an awakener."

Looking back, I realize that my dream of teaching was shaped not only by the kindness of those who encouraged me, but also by the moments when I learned what not to do. Correction without compassion can silence a child's voice, but encouragement can set it free. The worksheets I graded in my childhood bedroom were more than play; they were rehearsals for the kind of teacher I hoped to become—one who would awaken hidden strengths, nurture curiosity, and create a classroom where kindness was inseparable from learning.

But school was not always a safe place for a girl like me. In the tidy, conformist world of 1950s Midwestern towns, red hair, bifocal glasses, and practical brown stockings marked me as different. The town kids seemed to sense difference like wolves scenting blood.

"Hey, Carrot Top! Big Red! Woody Woodpecker!"

Their names bounced down the hallways, sing-song and sharp, like pebbles flicked at my neck. Being a farm girl only worsened it. Town kids walked in clean shoes and white stockings; I carried the smell of morning chores in my sleeves.

"Did you have to milk the cows before school?" they'd ask, pretending curiosity but smirking at the edges.

Every question was a tiny reminder: You don't belong here.

One moment is etched into me as if carved in stone. We were lining up for class, the girls straightening their skirts, smoothing the white stockings they all seemed to wear like a uniform. I stood in my sturdy brown ones—our "school stockings" because white ones were reserved for Sundays, as everyone on a farm understood why. A girl from town looked around theatrically. "We're all wearing white stockings. Look around this room!" Then she jabbed her finger at me. "Well, except for you. You look like you forgot to wash yours last night."

My jaw dropped. It felt heavy, as if I'd swallowed a stone. My eyes were wide, unblinking, as if I'd just been slapped. Heat rose up my neck. The room seemed to tilt for a second. I glanced at my friend—another farmer's daughter—whose blue eyes met mine with a mix of defiance and understanding. Her eyebrows lifted just slightly, a silent "Don't let them see you break." We smiled, a small rebellion, and stepped away from the mob.

Having farm friends was a life-saver: people who valued me without judgment, who didn't care that my dresses were hand-me-downs my mother had reworked from my aunt's castoffs. With them, I could laugh freely, unafraid of ridicule. They knew the rhythm of chores, the smell of hay, the satisfaction of hard work. They knew that stockings were not about fashion but about practicality, and that Sunday whites were too precious to scuff on weekday floors.

I was a light-skinned, freckled child who burned every time we went to the beach, a girl who never quite matched the polished look of the town kids. But slowly, through the sting of moments like that one, I learned something steadier than their cruelty. I learned not to swallow the limits others placed on me, and to see my own worth through the dust of the barn, the discipline of early mornings, and the kindness of those who truly saw me.

Rothsay had its unspoken hierarchies—farm versus town, white versus anyone who wasn't, Lutheran versus "other." Prejudice lived in the air we breathed, almost invisible, shaping who was welcomed and who was kept at arm's length. In those classrooms, amid freckles, brown stockings, and ridicule, a quiet resolve began to form. It taught me I could acknowledge pain without letting it define me, and that empowerment sometimes begins with a single moment of not looking away.

In a way, the cruelty of the city girls was a gift. It prepared me well to understand the racism to come—the turbulence of the 1960's, when prejudice would no longer be whispered in coatrooms but shouted in streets. The lessons of childhood were not wasted; they became the foundation for seeing injustice clearly and refusing to let silence be the final word.

The lessons of discrimination left their mark, shaping how I saw myself and the world around me. Yet even as those shadows lingered, change was happening closer to home. In the late 1950s, Dad transformed our old farmhouse from a place of outdoor plumbing and kerosene lamps into something that felt almost modern.

For years, our lives had been measured by the rhythm of chores and the dim glow of lanterns. Trips to the outhouse in the biting cold, the creak of the pump handle at dawn, the shadows that danced against plaster walls—all of it was simply the way things were.

And then, almost overnight, everything changed. Electric lights brightened rooms that had once been lit by flame. Downstairs, Dad added a long, open dining and living room with blond hardwood floors that glowed like honey in the afternoon sun, a coat closet that smelled of fresh-cut lumber, and a gigantic picture window that made the whole world outside feel close enough to touch. A new master bedroom and bath completed the addition, a luxury that seemed unimaginable only a few years before.

Between the kitchen and dining room, Dad cut a wide opening so Mom could pass food through—steaming plates of potatoes and roasts sliding easily from one room to the next. And in the living room, perched like royalty, sat our very first television. I can still remember the soft hum it made and the faint smell of warming tubes when it came to life. For a farm family used to radio voices drifting through static, the moving images felt like a miracle, a window into a wider world.

Upstairs, instead of dividing the original bedroom, Dad built two entirely new ones above the new living and dining area—fresh, clean spaces with smooth walls and, best of all, no more mice scampering inside them at night. My own room nestled beneath the dormer became my favorite place of all. The space was just big enough for my bunk bed, piled with heavy quilts Mom had sewn from old clothes and filled with soft cotton that smelled faintly of the cedar chest where they were stored. Built-in drawers climbed the walls on either side of the dormer, reaching nearly to the eaves, their wooden knobs cool to the touch on winter mornings.

That tiny dormer room became my refuge from the constant rhythm of farm life—the clang of milk pails, the lowing of cattle, the wind sifting through the cornfields. It was where I studied, where I dreamed, and where I first began to imagine the shape my future might take. The remodel was more than lumber and plaster; it was a declaration that change was possible, that even in the middle of farm fields, life could expand, modernize, and open toward something new.

The renovating marked a turning point: our family stepped into modern comforts just as the country itself was stepping into a new decade. Soon, the 1960s would demand their own lessons—of love, of loss, and of the widening world beyond the farm.

The 1960s: Awakening in Turbulence

By the time the 1960's arrived, the world felt as if it had shifted beneath our feet. What had once been whispered in classrooms now filled headlines and television screens. Civil rights marches, Vietnam protests, and the rise of new music all pressed against the boundaries of our small Minnesota town. For me, adolescence unfolded against this backdrop of turbulence, each personal awakening echoing the larger awakenings of the nation.

At school, the hierarchies I had felt in stockings and freckles seemed suddenly smaller compared to the divisions broadcast from beyond our town. On the evening news, I saw Black students facing jeers as they walked into newly integrated schools, their courage reminding me of the defiance I had once shared with a farm friend in a classroom line. The cruelty of childhood taunts had prepared me, in its own way, to recognize the injustice of prejudice when it appeared on a national stage.

Music carried the decade's pulse into our lives. Elvis had already shaken the edges of tradition, but now the Beatles, Bob Dylan, and Joan Baez filled radios with songs that spoke of change, rebellion, and longing. Their lyrics felt like invitations to imagine a world larger than Rothsay, one where voices could rise against war and inequality. I listened late at night, the hum of the farm quiet around me, and wondered what part I might play in that wider chorus.

The Vietnam War cast its own shadow. Boys I knew faced the draft, their futures tied to decisions made far from our classrooms. Some left quietly; others returned changed, carrying stories that unsettled the simplicity of farm life. Even in our small town, the war was impossible to ignore. It seeped into conversations, into the worried glances of parents, into the silence of those who had lost someone.

For girls, the turbulence was quieter but no less real. Expectations pressed hard: marry young, raise children, keep faith and modesty intact. I felt that my options were fixed and few; I could be a teacher, a secretary, or a nurse, but becoming a doctor or a lawyer felt entirely out of reach. Yet whispers of women's liberation began to reach us, carried in magazines and the occasional sermon warning against "worldly ideas." I felt the tension between tradition and possibility, between the silence I had grown up with and the voices beginning to demand more.

Even in Rothsay, the changes seeped in through small cracks. A neighbor's son returned from college with longer hair and sharper opinions. A cousin brought home a record that made my parents frown but made me lean closer. The church bulletin carried warnings about "modern temptations," but the youth group whispered about marches in faraway cities. The world was pressing in, and even the farm could not keep it out.

Looking back, the 1960s were not only a national upheaval but a personal one. They taught me that prejudice was not confined to classrooms, that silence could be broken, and that fortitude mattered as much in society as it did in childhood. The decade's turbulence became my awakening: a reminder that the world was larger, harsher, and more hopeful than I had ever imagined. And in its noise and shadows, I began to see the outlines of the woman I was becoming.

The Gopher Hunter's Wage

Even shaken by the turbulence of the 1960s, I kept moving—because farm life always offered the next challenge. One of those challenges came in the form of pocket gophers, whose little volcano mounds dotted the fields like miniature battle scars. Dad hated them: the mounds forced him to cut higher and nick his equipment, dulling blades and slowing work. For me, though, they meant opportunity. The county offered a penny for each back right foot, and for a child with a mind for cash, that was an irresistible job.

I learned to read the field like a map. Fresh, fluffed mounds meant a living burrow; older ones had hardened into useless humps. Kneeling, I dug with my fingers, cool crumbly soil slipping through my palms. The tunnel smelled of damp earth and a faint animal musk; every scrape brought up a new pocket of compacted dirt that took effort to pry free. I carried a small tin can for the "proofs," its lid rattling with each addition, the sound both grim and satisfying. Each penny felt like a tiny victory, a step toward buying something of my own.

The work was not glamorous. Dirt streaked my arms, grit lodged under my fingernails, and sometimes the burrows collapsed before I could set a trap. But there was a rhythm to it: dig, probe, set, wait. I felt a strange pride in knowing the land so closely, in recognizing the signs of life beneath the surface. It was a job that belonged to no one but me, a way to carve out independence in a world where most decisions were made by adults.

One afternoon I found what looked like a perfect tunnel and set to work clearing a place for the trap. My hand probed deeper, felt the packed wall give way—and something smooth, cool, and suddenly alive squirmed against my fingers. A lizard, slick and frantic, twisted in my grip. I jumped back, heart thudding, and the trap idea vanished along with my courage. "Yikes!" I yelled, flinging it gently aside. The lizard flattened and darted away into the grass, leaving me shaken and laughing at my own fright.

After that, I never did much gopher hunting. I'd still lean toward a little pocket money, but I picked tasks where the surprises didn't wriggle. The pennies I earned were quickly spent, but the lesson stayed: farm work was full of hidden challenges, some you could plan for and some that startled you out of your skin. In its own way, gopher hunting taught me grit—the kind that comes from facing the unexpected, even when it scurries away faster than you can catch it.

Farm life had its own rhythm—pennies earned from gopher hunting, chores that filled the days, and small victories that made me feel capable. Yet shadows never disappeared for long. Even as I grew older, they returned in familiar ways, reminding me that survival was never guaranteed. I learned again how quickly health could vanish and how easily opportunity could be stolen.

By the time I reached high school, the challenges shifted.

The fields still demanded labor, but the classroom demanded identity. I was no longer just a farm child chasing pennies; I was a teenager navigating expectations, friendships, and the fragile balance between health and opportunity. Illness returned like an unwelcome visitor, stealing breath and vitality, reminding me that the strength to keep going was not only about facing gophers or chores—it was about facing myself.

High school was a place where futures were imagined, but mine often felt uncertain. Each bout of sickness carried the threat of falling behind, of being overlooked, of losing the chance to step into the world beyond Rothsay. The lessons of fortitude I had learned in the fields now had to guide me thorough my own body, my own ambitions.

The Speech I Never Gave

The illness never truly left me. Even after that first terrifying bout in childhood, pneumonia seemed to linger like a shadow, waiting for the right moment to strike again. Years later, in high school, I was part of the Declam team, eager to prove myself in competition. I had practiced my speech until the words felt etched into me, rehearsing in front of the mirror, imagining the proud faces of my parents in the audience. Fergus Falls was the destination—the very town whose clinic had once turned my mother away when I was gasping for air as a child. This time, I was determined to arrive not as a patient but as a competitor.

That morning, Dad drove me only as far as the highway, two miles from our farm. I don't know why he couldn't take me all the way to school to meet the bus, but I stood there in the biting winter air, waiting for my ride. A friend had promised to tell the driver where to pick me up. I never saw the bus. The road stretched empty, the cold pressing in like a living thing. My breath came sharp and shallow, each exhale a puff of white against the frozen air.

The cold seeped into me quickly. My hands stiffened, my feet went numb, and soon my whole body felt frozen. Panic rose in me—no cell phones in the 1950s, no easy way to call for help. I knew I couldn't wait any longer. Frantically, I decided to walk the mile to my grandmother's house. Each step was heavy, each breath cut like glass against my lungs. By the time I reached her door, I was trembling and weak, my body already surrendering to the illness that had been waiting for its chance.

Grandma wasted no time. She called my parents, and they rushed me to the Fergus Falls hospital. Once again, pneumonia had claimed me. Once again, I was confined to a hospital bed, missing out on the contest, my speech left unspoken. The sterile smell of disinfectant filled the room, the sheets stiff and white against my fevered skin. Nurses moved briskly, their voices clipped, while I lay suspended between ambition and fragility. Outside, classmates were reciting their speeches, stepping into the spotlight I had longed for. Inside, I was fighting for breath.

I remember staring at the ceiling tiles, each square a reminder of the words I had memorized but would never deliver. The speech lived inside me, rehearsed and ready, but illness had stolen the stage. My voice was silenced not by fear but by fever, not by doubt but by disease.

Looking back, I see how these repeated brushes with illness shaped me. They taught me the fragility of life, but also the grit that comes from surviving. Pneumonia stole opportunities—a childhood of carefree play, a high school competition where I might have shone—but it also gave me perspective. I learned early that health could not be taken for granted, that determination mattered as much as talent. Standing on that frozen road, abandoned by the bus, I felt the same helplessness I had as a child gasping for air. Yet both times, I survived.

Survival became a kind of quiet victory, a reminder that even when my body betrayed me, I could endure. Later in life, when challenges came—whether in school, work, or relationships—I carried that knowledge with me: I had faced pneumonia, twice, and lived. The contest was lost, but the lesson remained: sometimes the ability to persevere is the truest performance of all.

Illness had stolen my chance to stand on stage, leaving me with silence instead of applause. Yet even as pneumonia reminded me of fragility, adolescence carried its own defiance. The world was changing—music pulsed through radios, dances filled gymnasiums, and first love stirred in unexpected places. If sickness had taught me endurance, Elvis and my first love taught me rebellion, joy, and the thrill of claiming my own voice.

Blue Suede Dreams

By the late 1950s, Elvis Presley's voice was everywhere—on radios in kitchens, jukeboxes in diners, and whispered about in church circles where his swiveling hips were considered scandalous. For me, his music was a revelation. The beat was bold, the lyrics daring, and the sound carried a freedom that felt like it belonged to my generation alone. When I listened late at night, the farm quiet around me, I felt a spark of independence, as if the world beyond Rothsay was calling.

Adults frowned at Elvis, shaking their heads at his records and warning that "good girls" shouldn't listen. But for us teenagers, his voice was a secret permission slip. He gave us rhythm when the world demanded restraint, daring when the town preached modesty. His music was a doorway, and I stepped through it every time I turned the dial on the radio.

First love arrived with its own pattern. He was a boy from school, a twin who had moved to our town in second grade. I first sat with him in the coat room, reading side by side—a quiet beginning that would later grow into glances across classrooms, notes passed in folded paper triangles, and the nervous excitement of phone calls made from the kitchen wall phone where privacy was impossible. His smile was quick, his laugh contagious, and my heart raced in ways that felt both exhilarating and terrifying, a new kind of vulnerability that no illness could prepare me for.

Back then, phone calls were never truly private. Several households shared a single line, each with its own ringing pattern. Our love was carried over wires that crackled with gossip, where neighbors could pick up and listen in. Even so, those late-night calls—hushed voices, laughter, promises—remain some of my most cherished memories.

The halls between classes became our stage—lockers slamming shut, laughter echoing, the faint smell of pencil shavings and cafeteria food lingering in the air. My locker was plastered with Elvis Presley's face, his grin daring the world to tell me no. He was my secret rebellion, my soundtrack to teenage love.

Daryl and I lingered there after lunch, leaning against the cool metal, trading jokes and glances that felt like promises. We weren't breaking rules exactly, but we weren't rushing off to class either. The principal's heels clicked down the hallway, her eyes narrowing as she passed. No words—just that stern look, the kind that could freeze a smile mid-laugh. Sometimes she gave us the silent treatment, as if ignoring us might erase the sweetness of our stolen minutes.

Still, those moments mattered. They were ours. Until the day she opened my locker and stripped it bare, tossing every Elvis photo into the trash. I stood stunned, devastated. My favorite singer—gone. It wasn't just paper she threw away; it felt like she was trying to silence the music, the romance, the rebellion that lived in those halls.

Looking back, Elvis gave me permission to move differently, to feel differently, to imagine a life beyond the narrow expectations of town hierarchies and farm chores. First love gave me courage to risk vulnerability. Together, they taught me that adolescence was not only about surviving shadows—it was about claiming joy, even if only in stolen minutes by a locker door.

But courage in adolescence often came tangled with fear. Sometimes it showed up not in whispered notes or posters tucked inside lockers, but in the trembling hands of a girl behind the wheel of a car. I was sixteen, terrified, and determined—all at once. The Pelican Rapids versus Rothsay basketball game was the event of the week, and every friend I had, including Daryl, was going. My only obstacle? I'd have to drive there alone, something that felt far more dangerous than any rivalry on the court. Daryl had to share the car with his twin brother that night.

My parents were hosting their weekly card night, the house warm with laughter while the buttery scent of fresh popcorn drifted through every room. I slipped the keys from the bowl by the door, hoping no one noticed the way my hand shook. Outside, the winter air hit me in the face, sharp enough to make my eyes water. It felt like a bad omen.

I climbed into our car, took a deep breath, and turned the key. The engine's rumble did nothing to steady me. I shifted into reverse. One second of confidence—then metal kissed metal.

The sound was almost delicate, a slow, scraping confession. I looked over my shoulder to see the long, unforgiving stripe I had carved into our friends' car. My chest tightened. Every instruction I had ever been given about responsibility vanished under the weight of panic.

Instead of going inside to tell them, I fled.

I drove to the gym on autopilot, knuckles white, breath

shallow, heart racing the entire way. I sat on the bleachers, but I didn't see a single play. The scoreboard might as well have been blank. The only thing I saw was that ruined car. The only thing I heard was that terrible scrape.

The next morning, Dad came into my room. No anger. No disappointment written on his face—just calm.

"Tell me what happened," he said softly.

And I did. Tears streaming, voice breaking, I told him everything. I braced myself for the consequences.

Instead, he said, "It could have been so much worse. I'm thankful no one was hurt."

In that moment, I understood something profound: grace is sometimes a greater teacher than punishment. His response carved a different kind of mark—one that stayed with me far longer than the scrape on that car. That quiet mercy didn't end my rebellion; it gave it room to grow.

Elvis was my private soundtrack, and first love was my secret rebellion. But rebellion cannot stay hidden forever. Of course, hanging out in the halls was only part of the story. Beyond the posters tucked inside lockers and whispered notes in classrooms, our lives spilled into roller rinks, drive-ins, and family kitchens. That's where dating began to shape us, teaching lessons of love, heartbreak, and belonging.

Rings, Rinks, and Drive-in Dreams

The sound of tires crunching on the gravel driveway meant only one thing: Daryl was bringing me home. Mom would already be in the kitchen, stirring a pan of sloppy joes she kept warm on the stove, waiting for us.

"You two must be hungry," she'd say with a smile, sliding buns onto plates as the savory aroma filled the room. Daryl would laugh, settling into a chair at our kitchen table, chatting easily with my parents as though he belonged there. I'd sit beside him. still glowing from the evening—roller skating, a drive-in movie, or a stop at Dairyland—and feel the comfort of being home, surrounded by family.

It was a ritual as steady as curfews and class rings: the date ended not with silence or separation, but with food, conversation, and the gentle folding of young love into the pattern of family life.

Dating in the 1950s and early 60's carried a sense of formality and ritual. Boys initiated the pursuit, arriving at the girl's home to pick her up, and ensuring she was back by curfew. They paid for the evening and made all the arrangements, while girls were expected to be reserved, polite, and punctual.

The idea of *"going steady"* was the dream. Couples exchanged tokens of commitment—class rings, pins, or bracelets—as symbols of exclusivity. When he slipped his class ring onto my finger, heavy and cold, it felt more permanent than any promise. My palms dampened and my heart fluttered like a hummingbird against my ribs. The world faded, the noise of other boys, other possibilities, all silenced by that simple silver band. I wore his ring, proudly, twisting it on my finger during class, dreaming of a future life together.

Later that summer, though, he surprised me.

"*I think we should give these back,*" he said quietly, holding out my ring.

I stared at him, stunned. "*What do you mean? Are you breaking up with me?*"

He shook his head, but didn't explain. I handed his ring back, my heart sinking. For a week, I didn't hear from him—he was working on his grandparents' farm, twenty-five miles away.

I remember those days so clearly. I would sit at the kitchen table, staring at my plate, the food untouched. My stomach felt knotted, and even the thought of swallowing made me queasy. Mom noticed right away—each meal I skipped only deepened her worry. One evening, she finally said, "We're going to the doctor. I can't just sit here and watch you waste away." I didn't protest. I didn't have the strength.

The doctor's office smelled faintly antiseptic, the kind of place where answers are supposed to live. I sat on the crinkling paper of the exam table, my hands folded in my lap, while Mom explained how I hadn't been eating.

The doctor turned to me, his tone gentle, but direct. "Tell me," he said, "what's been going on? Any changes in your life?" I hesitated, but eventually admitted that I thought my boyfriend and I were breaking up. The words felt heavy, like admitting them made the fear more real.

The doctor leaned back, nodding with understanding. "That explains a lot," he said. "What you're experiencing isn't a stomach illness. It's your body reacting to emotional stress. Anxiety and sadness can shut down your appetite. It's not uncommon for people to feel like they can't eat when they're overwhelmed."

Mom's eyes softened with relief, though her concern didn't vanish. For me, the explanation was both startling and comforting. I realized my body wasn't betraying me—it was reflecting the turmoil inside. The hunger I had lost wasn't about food at all; it was about heartbreak.

Walking out of the clinic, I realized that sometimes the body tells the story we're too afraid to speak, revealing the quiet devastation of believing someone you care for might leave.

When school started again, Daryl finally told me the truth.

"It wasn't about us," he said, looking sheepish. "Your ring kept bending while I was working. I didn't want to ruin it."

Relief washed over me, though I couldn't help but laugh at the absurdity. What had felt like heartbreak was really just a bent ring.

Dates often involved groups of couples piling into cars and heading to popular spots—roller skating rinks, bowling alleys, ice cream parlors, or drive-in theaters.

I loved roller skating. My metal strap-on skates clamped over my leather shoes, and I'd glide in circles to the sound of Buddy Holly, Elvis Presley, and Chuck Berry blaring through the speakers. Halfway through the night, the announcer's voice would boom:

"Reverse direction!"

We'd all laugh as the crowd shifted, arms swinging, legs kicking forward in rhythm. My hair flew behind me, and for those moments, I felt utterly free.

Drive-in theaters were another favorite. We'd pull into the lot, clip the tinny metal speaker onto the car window, and settle in under the stars. The sound crackled, but it didn't matter. The flickering light from the screen illuminated rows of cars, and during intermission, we'd watch the dancing hot dogs and popcorn ads urging us to visit the snack bar. Sometimes, impatient horns honked at the screen, adding to the chorus of summer nights.

And when the movie ended, the night didn't; we'd head straight to the car-hop stands that were buzzing with energy. Dairyland opened in Fergus Falls in 1955, and it quickly became *the* place to go. Car hops in crisp uniforms skated up to windows, balancing trays of hamburgers, fries, and ice cream sundaes. The trays clipped neatly onto the car window, and the air was filled with chatter, laughter, and the hum of radios playing upbeat tunes.

"Two chocolate malts and a basket of fries," a car hop would say, handing over the tray with a smile.

We'd eat, talk, and watch the steady stream of cars pulling in and out, each one part of the pulse of teenage life.

Summers often meant weekends at Daryl's family cabin. We'd take turns water skiing, cheering each other on. Daryl was graceful on one ski, cutting across the wake with ease. I tried once, only to flip spectacularly into the lake.

"You'll get it next time!" he shouted from the boat, laughing. Not wanting to lose my contact lenses, I never tried again.

We cooled off by jumping from the dock, splashing into the water, or floating lazily in the sun. Lunch was simple—hamburgers on the grill, hot dogs roasted over the fire, marshmallows toasted until golden. Evenings ended with s'mores, fireflies flickering in the dark, and conversations under the stars.

Winters brought a different pattern. I was often invited to the Hauger home for Sunday dinner. With six children and their girlfriends, the house was alive with chatter and laughter. Daryl's mother always prepared a feast—mashed potatoes, gravy, turkey, chicken, ham, or roast beef, with vegetables from her garden and warm rolls fresh from the oven.

"Don't forget dessert," she'd say, setting down pies or cakes, while the cookie jar in the freezer was always stocked with chocolate chip cookies.

Their home had a television long before ours, and Daryl's father, Gerald, could often be found in his favorite chair, pipe in hand. The polished briar bowl glowed faintly as he drew in a puff, the sweet, woody scent of tobacco drifting through the room. Smoke curled upward in lazy spirals, catching the lamplight as he leaned back, calm and steady, watching the screen or lifting his video recorder to capture the family gathered around him. He rarely spoke of his years flying bombers in World War II, though the weight of those experiences seemed to hang quietly in the room, unspoken but present.

Daryl and his twin brother Dayle were born while their father was overseas, leading missions as a bomber pilot. The war had shaped Gerald's life, and in ways we didn't yet understand, it had shaped Daryl's too. At the time, I only knew the warmth of Sunday dinners and the comfort of family chatter. But another war, years later, would reach into our lives and alter the course of our story.

Dating then was a blend of ritual and innocence. Rings exchanged, curfews kept, meals waiting at home—it all carried a sense of structure and community. Families were part of the cadence of romance. When Daryl brought me home after a date, Mom always had something warm waiting on the stove, her quiet way of welcoming us home.

The kitchen filled with the savory smell of tomato and beef, the sound of laughter, and the comfort of knowing love wasn't just between two people—it was folded into the family. My parents welcomed Daryl, and his presence became part of our household routine.

That kind of family involvement was common then. Parents met the boy at the door, siblings teased, and Sunday dinners were shared with extended families. Dating wasn't only about the couple—it was about how they fit into the larger circle of home and community.

Today, dating often unfolds in private spaces—text

messages, dating apps, coffee shops far from home. Families may not meet a partner until much later, and the rituals of curfews, shared meals, and parental oversight have largely faded. Independence has grown, but sometimes at the cost of connection.

Looking back, I realize how grounding it was to have family woven into those early relationships. The sloppy joes waiting on the stove, the chatter around Daryl's family table, the laughter at the cabin—all of it gave dating a sense of belonging. Love wasn't just about two people finding each other; it was about two families opening their doors, their kitchens, and their hearts.

Yet beneath the warmth of those evenings, there were shadows we didn't fully see. Gerald's silence carrying a weight I didn't understand, a heaviness that would make sense only years later, when the world changed again and took Daryl with it in ways none of us could have imagined.

For now, though, the soundtrack was Buddy Holly and Elvis, the glow of drive-in screens, and the comfort of sloppy joes at midnight. Those nights were the heartbeat of my teenage years. If Elvis and first love belonged to the shadows, Homecoming became my spotlight.

Under the Gymnasium Lights

If Elvis and first love were my private rebellion, Homecoming was my public awakening. The week of Homecoming in the 1950s felt like a festival, a rare moment when our small town seemed to swell with pride and possibility. Floats rattled down Main Street, tractors pulling wagons dressed in crepe paper and hay bales, cheerleaders waving from the back of pickup trucks. The marching band blared brass and drumbeats that echoed against storefronts, and candy rained down into the eager hands of children darting along the sidewalks. Farmers leaned against their trucks, shopkeepers stood in doorways, and for a few days Rothsay felt larger than itself, united together by pride and anticipation.

Inside the school, the gym buzzed with energy. Streamers crisscrossed the rafters, balloons bobbed against the ceiling, and the air was thick with perfume, floor wax, and school spirit. Teachers smiled more easily, students whispered predictions, and the pep rally carried the electricity of possibility.

I never expected to be part of the spotlight. On pep rally day, I slipped into an aqua-blue chiffon-over-taffeta dress, its can-can petticoat bouncing with every step. My hands trembled as I smoothed the skirt, certain I wouldn't win. I even told Mom to stay home—why let her watch me lose?

When my name was called, the gym erupted. A crown settled on my head, and for a moment I felt both stunned and weightless. The applause washed over me, erasing the sting of nicknames and the ache of pneumonia. For once, I was not the farm girl marked by difference—I was the queen, lifted high by the voices of classmates who had once doubted me. I caught sight of Mom slipping quietly into the back of the gym, her eyes shining, and I realized she had come anyway. Her smile steadied me, reminding me that even victories are sweeter when shared.

That night, Daryl and I went to the sock hop after the game. The gym floor was slick with wax, shoes kicked off at the door, laughter bouncing against the walls. We danced in stocking feet, careful to honor the rules of our religious culture, which warned that dancing could tempt us toward sin. Even in college, the ban lingered, but that night the music and laughter felt like freedom wrapped in caution. Elvis's voice spilled from the speakers, daring us to move differently, and we did—our joy a quiet defiance against rules that tried to contain us.

Looking back, Homecoming was more than a crown or a dance. It was a turning point, a moment when private rebellion became public recognition. The girl who had once been singled out for red hair, freckles and brown stockings now stood in chiffon, crowned and celebrated. It was proof that joy could triumph over shadows, that belonging could be claimed, and that adolescence held not only trials but victories worth remembering.

Homecoming crowned me with a moment of joy, a public

recognition that balanced years of shadows. But adolescence does not linger forever. The music faded, the streamers came down, and soon life asked something more of me than dances and rebellion. My next awakening came not in a gymnasium but in the quiet rooms of responsibility—my first full-time job, caring for someone who needed me, while living under the steady roof of my grandmother.

Responsibility and Grandma's Roof

My first full-time job was not glamorous, but it was unforgettable. One summer in my late high-school years, I was hired to care for a handicapped person, a task that demanded patience, compassion, and a steadiness I was still learning to carry. The work was intimate and humbling—helping with meals, guiding through daily routines, listening when words came slowly or not at all. Each day reminded me that independence was not something everyone could claim, and that dignity mattered most when life had stripped away ease.

I was caring for the neighbor across the street from Grandma's. She was confined to her bed, and while her husband worked, I cooked her meals and kept the house in order. It was there I learned the quiet art of mending socks—my fingers fumbling at first, the fabric stretched tight over a wooden darning ball, the needle flashing in and out until the hole slowly disappeared. Each stitch felt like proof that I could make something whole again.

I also learned the patience of ironing. With no steam or temperature control, the iron demanded constant attention—too cool and the wrinkles stayed, too hot and the fabric scorched. I dampened collars and cuffs, pressing carefully, listening to the faint hiss as the heat met cloth. The rhythm of ironing became almost meditative: the sweep of the iron, the release of wrinkles, the satisfaction of crisp lines.

Cleaning her house filled the rest of my days. I dusted shelves lined with family photographs, polished the worn wood of the dining table, and scrubbed floors until they gleamed. At week's end, fifteen dollars waited in my hand. It wasn't just money—it was independence, a reward for work that taught me skills and gave me the gift of staying at Grandma's Monday through Friday in the summer.

I stayed at Grandma's during that time, her house a place of comfort and constancy. The rooms smelled faintly of coffee and starch, the kitchen always warm with bread or soup simmering on the stove. At night, I lay in the upstairs bedroom, the quilt heavy across me, listening to the tick of the clock and the creak of the old house settling. The wallpaper was faded, patterned with tiny roses, and the dresser drawers stuck when pulled too quickly. Grandma's presence was steady, her quiet grace a model for the patience I tried to bring to my work.

The job was demanding, but it taught me more than any classroom. I learned that care is not only physical—it is emotional, a willingness to sit in silence, to offer presence when solutions are few. I learned that responsibility is not about age but about choice: the choice to show up, to keep showing up, even when the work is hard. And I learned that independence, the very thing I longed for as a teenager, was something fragile, something precious, something worth protecting in others as well as myself.

Looking back, that season feels like a hinge between

adolescence and adulthood. Elvis and Homecoming had given me joy and rebellion; pneumonia had taught me fragility. But caring for another person taught me maturity. Under Grandma's roof, I began to understand that life was not only about claiming freedom—it was about carrying responsibility, about offering strength when someone else could not. It was the quiet beginning of the adult I was becoming.

Those summer weeks at Grandma's marked the end of one season of my life and the quiet beginning of another. Caring for someone else taught me patience; earning my own money gave me a sense of independence; and living under Grandma's roof revealed the constancy of steady love. I remember evenings on the porch, Grandma humming hymns while I shelled peas into a bowl, and the air heavy with the scent of lilacs. In those small rituals, something lasting took shape—an understanding that adulthood was not only about striving, but about care freely given.

That summer taught me responsibility, the kind you can only learn by doing. Care, steadiness, and service became habits rather than ideals. When autumn arrived, I felt ready—not certain, but grounded—to step beyond Rothsay and the familiar rhythms of farm and family. I carried Grandma's quiet lessons with me as the world began to widen, trusting they would hold even when everything else changed.

PART III: JOURNEYS AND CROSSROADS

Horizons widened as I left home, carrying the roots of childhood into lecture halls, hurried vows, and distant lands. These years became a crossroads of love, vocation, and discovery—where memory anchored me even as new journeys unfolded.

Degrees and Diamond Rings

Long before I packed a suitcase or truly left home, my world began to widen in quieter ways. The first widening came that summer I was chosen by our local American Legion Auxiliary to attend Girls' State—a week immersed in ritual, rhetoric, and unexpected responsibility. I arrived proud but apprehensive, stepping into a world of structured patriotism where every morning began with a crisp flag ceremony and the rhythmic comfort of the Pledge of Allegiance. We were immediately sorted into fictional "cities" and opposing "parties," a social experiment in instant belonging and performance.

The structure was comforting at first—flags raised, rules explained, roles assigned—but it didn't take long for ceremony to give way to performance. Campaigns began, and the air shifted. Confidence became currency; volume became authority. I found myself swept into a municipal race, expected to persuade, negotiate, and assert myself in ways that felt unfamiliar and revealing.

My time campaigning for a municipal office was a crucible. I remember the metallic taste of fear as I delivered a stiff, rehearsed speech beneath the bright, unforgiving gymnasium lights. While I struggled to summon confidence, my peers radiated it—their sharp elbows, their hunger for the gavel—and I felt a profound dissonance between the performance required for public office and my quiet self. I watched others thrive on the competitive current, engaging in the necessary horse-trading of legislative sessions and the sometimes cynical art of debate.

That week at Girls' State was the most unexpected gift: not because it sparked a love for policy, but because it clarified my soul's deepest aversion. I realized I didn't want to argue about the mechanics of a system; I wanted to shape the people who would one day inherit it. The cacophony of the campaign hall faded, replaced by the quiet, resonant certainty that my true calling, my authentic self, belonged in a classroom, not a statehouse. The experience didn't make me a politician; it forged my identity as a future teacher.

That certainty followed me home, settling quietly into my final year of high school. I returned with a sharper sense of purpose, attentive to where my energy flowed and where it resisted. By the time graduation approached, college no longer felt like an abstract next step but a deliberate one. Concordia College in Moorhead became the place where that inward knowing could be tested and shaped—where my longing to teach would move from instinct to intention.

The science labs were where I felt most alive. Biology, zoology, and botany opened windows into worlds I had never seen. Dissecting a cat in biology was unforgettable—not only for the lessons in anatomy, but for the pungent smell of formaldehyde that clung to my hands, clothes, and hair long after I left the lab. It was overwhelming, yet strangely fascinating, a hands-on reminder of how similar the muscles and organs of animals were to our own. At the time, none of us thought about the ethics of it. Cats were plentiful in shelters, rarely adopted, and often euthanized. Their bodies became part of our education, a sobering reality I only reflected on years later.

Despite my love for science, I struggled in humanities. A perfectionist at heart, I was devastated by the "C" I earned. Greek mythology, the Parthenon, and ancient art felt distant and abstract to me. With no experiences beyond the United States, I had nothing to anchor the learning to, no background knowledge to help me make connections. No matter how hard I tried, an "A" in that class was beyond my reach. I remember sitting in the library, surrounded by heavy books filled with marble statues and ancient ruins, feeling as though I were staring into a world I could not touch. The gap between my farm upbringing and the grandeur of Greece felt insurmountable.

After my first year at Concordia, life shifted. My father suffered four heart attacks and had to retire from farming. The news came like a blow, reshaping everything. Without his financial support, I transferred to Moorhead State, taking summer classes so I could graduate early and support myself. The days were long—lectures in the morning, work in the afternoons, study late into the night—but determination carried me forward. I remember walking across campus with my arms full of books, the prairie wind tugging at my coat, exhaustion heavy but resolve stronger.

I graduated from Moorhead State in December of 1965, stepping into my long-held dream of teaching. By January of 1966, I was standing in front of my own classroom in

Fertile, Minnesota, teaching second graders—the dream I had carried since childhood finally becoming real. Their eager faces, the smell of chalk dust, the shuffle of little feet across the linoleum floor—all of it felt like the fulfillment of years of longing. I was no longer the student; I was the teacher.

I lived in a rented bedroom in the home of an elderly couple. Breakfast was always in their kitchen—toast, hot chocolate, sometimes oatmeal—and for other meals I walked down to the local restaurant. Supper was the hardest. I was so hungry by evening that I often ordered pie first, savoring the sweet bite before the main course arrived. My teacher's salary was $4,800 for the year, most of it spent on my first car: a baby-blue Chevy Malibu. Rent for my room was $50 a month. That winter was fierce. One storm buried my car to the roofline in a drift. I hired a group of high school boys to dig it out, their shovels clanging against the frozen metal, laughter rising in the bitter wind.

Just a few months later, in May of 1966, Daryl finished his own studies at Concordia. Like so many young men at the time, he lived under the shadow of the draft, which hung over our conversations and our future. Jobs were scarce for those who might be called up, and the fear of being left unemployed—or drafted without choice—pushed him to enlist in the Army. The war in Vietnam was no longer something we read about at a distance; it was appearing nightly on the evening news, in grainy footage of jungles and body counts, and in the names of boys not much older than we were.

He left for basic training at Fort Leonard Wood, Missouri, with a brave grin and the words, "See you in three years!" echoing in my ears. I smiled back because that was what he needed to see, even as my chest tightened and my throat burned with all the things I did not dare say. Three years felt impossibly long, and beneath my pride in his courage lay the quiet terror that those years—if they passed safely at all—might change us, or erase us, beyond recognition.

When Daryl told me he would see me in three years, I had nearly given up hope that our relationship could survive that long. In those days, few of us spoke openly about our fears; we carried them privately, listening to casualty numbers and wondering what they meant for our own lives. Yet as the feminist movement began to stir even in our small corner of the world, something in me began to stir as well. For the first time, I felt the faint but unmistakable sensation of being unsilenced. And when I wrote my name on the blackboard—Ms. *Flatin*—for the first time, I felt a spark of independence. "Ms." was still a new kind of title then, and choosing it felt like claiming a small corner of adulthood for myself, even as so much else remained uncertain.

But even as I was learning to stand on my own, our relationship was growing stronger. After only a few weeks, that certainty strengthened. His letters carried new promises. My sense of who I was—and who I hoped to become—was shifting.

That summer, Daryl came home on leave, and we immediately stood together at a jewelry counter, our reflections faintly visible in the glass as he asked me which diamond I liked. I chose a simple solitaire—one clear stone, no embellishment—because it felt honest and timeless, a single light meant to stand on its own. He worried it was too small, but I didn't. The size was never the point. What mattered was what it represented: a promise made quietly, without flourish, in the middle of so much uncertainty.

I don't remember exactly how he gave it to me—whether there was a speech or a question, whether my hands trembled or my voice caught—but I do remember the weight of it on my finger, and how its sparkle felt like a tether to the boy who had once lingered by my locker, now a man moving steadily toward a future neither of us could fully see. Soon after, he called from advanced training with a request: could we marry in October, before his orders came through, knowing Vietnam was a possibility? I said "yes," and began planning a wedding at my church for October 1. I can still picture the lists I made—guest names scribbled in neat columns, fabric swatches tucked into envelopes, hymns chosen for the ceremony—as if careful planning might hold the world steady.

Life seemed to be unfolding just as I had dreamed—a scholarship, the start of my teaching career, and a diamond ring from the boy I loved. With Daryl's call from advanced training, the promise of marriage felt like the natural next step, a moment to anchor our future before the uncertainty of military orders. I planned the October wedding with hope and determination, never suspecting how quickly those plans would be tested.

The Wedding That Almost Wasn't

At 22, I was teaching second graders in Fertile, Minnesota, finally living the dream I'd carried since childhood, with more hope than experience to guide me. My parents, Arnold and Thelma, were proud; Daryl, just 21 and freshly trained as an Army clerk typist, was the steady, gentle presence with whom I wanted to spend my life. We were young, deeply in love, and convinced that commitment itself could carry us forward.

Daryl's three-day pass felt like a small miracle, a window of time just big enough to hold our wedding ... or so we believed. I thought of the diamond on my finger then, how something so small could be shaped by pressure into something made to last. We trusted that those few days would be enough, that if we held them carefully, they would hold us in return.

That Friday evening, I was carefully pressing the delicate, tulle, elbow-length veil I'd borrowed from my dear friend Marilyn, my "something borrowed," chosen with all the optimism of a bride-to-be. As I guided the iron along the fabric, it suddenly snagged. A sharp hiss. A tiny hole! My heart ached, and the tears flowed faster than I could stop them.

"Mom!" I cried. "I have to get to Fergus Falls before the stores close!"

With only one shop that might carry a veil, I drove the twenty miles to Norby's, heart pounding. Then I saw it—perched on a mannequin at the last second, a moment that felt guided by some unseen hand of fate.

That night, under the familiar dormer window of my childhood bedroom, I curled beneath the quilt Grandma had sewn for me. I tried to quiet my mind by imagining the townspeople of little Rothsay preparing for our wedding. The pastor rehearsing his message. Dresses and suits laid out. Flowers delivered. The smell of scalloped potatoes and ham filling the church kitchen. I pictured Daryl traveling toward me, steady and sure. I let myself rest in the belief that everything was falling into place. In my head, I wasn't merely waiting for my day; I was waiting for the beginning of "forever."

The next morning—October 1, 1966—arrived soft and golden, with light filtering through bare branches and the familiar sounds of bacon sizzling in the pan. As I savored a mug of rich, steaming hot chocolate, I felt not nerves, but a quiet flutter of joy. Gratitude warmed me: for family, for friends, and for the love that had carried me to this moment.

Unexpectedly, the phone rang. Thoughts raced through my head! "Who could be calling? Is the organist sick? My matron of honor?"

"Good morning," I answered.

"Donna," Daryl said, his voice quivering. "CANCEL THE WEDDING!"

I froze.

My heart felt like it was going to burst. Tears streamed

down my face. Thoughts swirled in my head. My initial reaction was, "*This can't be happening!*" Daryl's pass had been approved by the army—everything was in place or so we thought. His twin brother, Dayle, and future sister-in-law, Marlyce, had driven from St. Louis to Fort Leonard Wood to escort him to Minnesota.

But just as they prepared to leave the day before the wedding, Daryl was told—without explanation—that his pass had been revoked. No details. No orders. Just a blunt, devastating halt. The Army was shifting assignments rapidly as troop numbers rose in Vietnam, and Daryl was suddenly swept into that tide. The detailed orders, he was told, would come the next day.

When reality set in, sadness and disbelief gripped me. How could it be that the day we planned to wed was in jeopardy? On the other end of the line, I heard him whimper for the first time since we started dating. Daryl's cracking voice responded, "Unless … you fly here and we get married at Fort Leonard Wood?"

After a few deep breaths, I didn't hesitate. "I'll find a way," I replied confidently.

That call changed everything! It was the pivot point between the wedding we had planned and the wedding we would improvise. From that moment on, the day became a race against time, against fog, against paperwork, against the Army itself.

Daryl promised to call back in an hour.

I sprang into action! I called the Fergus Falls Municipal Airport, Einar Mickelson Field, scrambling to secure a charter flight to Missouri. Only one plane could make the 600-mile trip in time and it was reserved by a physician from Graceville. In a stroke of kindness, he agreed to take a smaller aircraft so my pilot could use the twin-engine plane. In a New York minute, I handed over the $450 in exchange for a wedding ceremony far from that which was planned.

As Phyllis—my attendant by an unexpected turn of events—and I left my home, I was hardly dressed for a wedding, wearing my army-green wool "going-away" dress. Facing my stunned parents, I shouted, "CANCEL THE WEDDING! Phyllis and I will be back from Missouri in twelve hours!"

Afterward, my parents phoned my pastor to break the news. Hearing how disappointed everyone would be, he proposed an extraordinary idea. Let the wedding continue—*without the bride and groom!*

But nature had its own obstacles. What began as a clear, sunny dawn transformed into a landscape of soft, diffused light. Thick fog blanketed the runway swallowing it up. Phyllis, who also taught in Fertile, Minnesota, and I sat in silence, suspended in a world of white. Silence hung in the cockpit like a held breath. My heart pounded like the beating On a drum. I pressed my forehead to the cold glass, searching for any sign of movement, praying the fog would lift. Then—finally—a flicker. A distant orange light pierced the gloom. Slowly, the mist lifted. The pilot was cleared for takeoff!

At 9:15 a.m., *we were airborne.*

While Rothsay prepared for a wedding without us, Daryl's

day at Fort Leonard Wood, deep in the Missouri Ozarks, was unraveling as anticipated by the newly received orders. Although, October 1, 1966, began like any other day: reveille at 4:50 a.m., breakfast at 5:20, marching to Building 3, his training center, by 7:00 a.m. It was any thing but normal. He was ordered to report back at 4:00 p.m. to meet the bus enroute to McGuire Air Force Base in New Jersey. *Destination: Germany.*

Back at the barracks, Daryl stood in his Army Service Uniform, the gold trim on his dark blue coat catching the light as he moved. His trousers matched the coat, and the peaked cap sat squarely on his head, its brim shading his eyes. Spit-shined shoes completed the look. But the uniform only made the moment feel more surreal. His shoulders sagged. His eyes were red-rimmed and unfocused, as if staring through everything around him. His hands trembled as he folded and refolded the same pair of socks, unable to steady himself. The weight of the news pressed on him so heavily that even breathing seemed like an effort.

When Daryl and Marlyce arrived they found him sitting on the edge of the bunk, elbows on his knees, head bowed. He looked up at them with a hollow expression—part disbelief, part heartbreak, part exhaustion from packing his standard gear—camouflage uniform, field jacket, and boots. The strong, steady Daryl they knew had been replaced by a young man caught between duty and love, with no power to choose either.

Together they turned in Daryl's equipment before heading toward the Fort Leonard Wood airport.

Daryl tried to coordinate our landing, but Fort Leonard Wood's airstrip required a two-way radio and a formal flight plan. Redirected to Rolla's Municipal Airfield instead, he began scrambling to make sense of Missouri marriage laws.

First stop was the chapel on base. The chaplain informed Daryl we needed a Missouri license and blood tests. Legal assistance confirmed it. He had assumed our Minnesota license would work in Missouri. It wouldn't. Time was running out, and the Army clock ticked louder with every passing minute.

Daryl rushed to the Fort Leonard Wood Hospital for his blood test, then immediately called the Waynesville county clerk. She couldn't stay past noon and warned him of Missouri's mandatory three-day waiting period—unless a judge agreed to waive it.

Next, Daryl phoned the Rolla County Clerk. He was already on his way out of the courthouse for lunch, but agreed to return and process the marriage license if Daryl could secure a judicial waiver in time.

The judge was skeptical. He even hung up once, convinced Daryl was just a lonesome GI eager to marry a girl he'd barely met—not one of two childhood sweethearts with years of shared history. When the line went dead, Daryl stared at the phone, knowing time—and authority—were slipping through his fingers. He called again, more careful now, pressing urgency into calm words. The judge listened, unmoved, as if he'd heard some version of this story before. Finally, after a long pause, he relented—not with encouragement, but with a challenge—and gave Daryl his address.

Blood test in hand, Daryl and his crew drove to Salm Avenue, found the judge's house, and received the signed waiver. From there, they raced to the courthouse, guided by a local they'd picked up along the way.

The clerk's office was locked when they arrived, but fate intervened. The superintendent of schools, Mr. Bell, happened to be nearby.

"I'll help you call the clerk," he said. "And if you need someone to officiate..." He paused, then smiled. "I can do that too. I'm an ordained Baptist minister."

Relieved that the puzzle pieces were finally falling into place, Daryl asked, "How far is the Rolla airport?"

"Thirteen miles," Mr. Bell replied.

Daryl's heart sank. A tightness gripped his chest as the minutes ticked by. *Would my bride-to-be arrive in time?*

At 12:30 p.m., as Daryl waited anxiously at Rolla's airport, he spotted a small plane descending.

"I hope Donna and Phyllis are on board," he said, not expecting this to be the case.

It was.

The chartered plane dipped onto the runway, engines humming their last note before silence. As the door swung open, Missouri's damp air rushed in—heavier, thicker than the crisp northern wind I'd left behind. My heels struck the metal steps in a staccato rhythm, echoing across the hushed airfield. And then I saw him.

The world collapsed to a single frame: his muted blue

uniform, his arms outstretched, waiting. I broke into a run, a blur of green against the tarmac, until his embrace lifted me, spun me, and held me fast. Tears blurred the edges of everything but him.

No sooner had we caught our breath than urgency pulled us onward. We sped to Rolla, straight to the hospital—the blood test still undone. The lab stood empty. The X-ray tech dialed the technician, but no answer. Each step felt like a race against time, each delay another wall in our path. We waited. I paced. Daryl tried again, the phone pressed tight, hope straining against silence.

"She's coming," he said, gripping my hand.

At 1:55 the lab technician finally appeared, and my stomach tightened. We were already behind, and every minute felt like it was slipping through our fingers. She didn't seem to feel the same urgency; her movements were calm, practiced, almost serene. I watched the clock over her shoulder as she swabbed my arm with cold rubbing alcohol. The smell hit me first—sharp, clinical—and for a moment I wondered if the sting on my skin was from the alcohol or from my own impatience.

The needle went in quickly, a small pinch, nothing dramatic, but I found myself holding my breath anyway. I could see the dark ribbon of blood filling the tube, and all I could think was, "Hurry. Please hurry." She removed the needle, pressed gauze to the spot, and secured it with a stretchy bandage as if we had all the time in the world.

Fifteen minutes later my skin had already sealed itself, my body doing its quiet work while the rest of my life felt like it was speeding out of control. The test would take an hour—an hour we didn't have. Daryl was already dialing Mr. Bell. "Meet us at the courthouse," he urgently announced.

Dayle and Marlyce raced back to the hospital for the results while Daryl and I filled out the paperwork for the marriage license. The clerk made a mistake. He started over. We held our breath.

Ten minutes later, Dayle and Marlyce burst into the courthouse with the test results, breathless and flushed from hurrying. The clerk stamped the final form and just like that, the license was complete. We rushed upstairs to a small, windowless office tucked at the end of a narrow hallway.

The room felt more like a storage space than a place where lives were joined—sterile white walls, a metal desk pushed against one side, a humming fluorescent light that flickered every few seconds. A single American flag stood in the corner, its fabric slightly dusty, and a stack of legal folders sat neatly on a chair as if someone had just stepped out for lunch. It was not the setting I had imagined for my wedding day, yet it was the only place in the world I wanted to be.

Mr. Bell, the justice of the peace, greeted us with a warm, steady presence that softened the harshness of the room. Daryl stood beside me in his Army Service Uniform, the gold trim catching the light each time he shifted his weight. I wore my simple going-away dress, still creased from travel. Dayle, Marlyce, and Phyllis formed a small semicircle around us—our impromptu wedding party.

Mr. Bell opened his worn leather binder and, in his gentle voice asked, *"Do you, Donna, take Daryl ..."*

The words echoed slightly off the bare walls, making the moment feel both intimate and monumental. My voice trembled as I answered. Daryl squeezed my hand—firm, certain, grateful.

At 2:55 p.m., in that plain courthouse office, we were pronounced husband and wife! But even then, the clock ticked. Mr. Bell made a mistake on the Marriage Certificate. He tried to erase it. We all stood there, silently pleading for speed. He finished it ... finally. We thanked him, snapped a few photos, and raced back to Fort Leonard Wood. We arrived with 20 minutes to spare. Just long enough to hold hands, take a breath, and say goodbye with a hug that would need to last until we would see each other again in eight months.

At 4:00 p.m., the bus pulled away, carrying my new husband toward Germany. I stood there watching it go, tears blurring the outline of the man I had promised to love for the rest of my life.

When the bus disappeared completely, a strange quiet settled around me. The whirlwind—the flight, the blood tests, the courthouse vows, the scramble against the Army's clock—had all happened so fast. Now there was only stillness, the echo of our vows lingering in my heart, and the ache of a goodbye far too soon. It wasn't the wedding we spent months planning—but it was our wedding. *Unpolished, unexpected, unforgettable.*

On the plane back to Minnesota, I sank into my cramped

seat beside Phyllis and tried to catch my breath. I was newly married, yet already separated from Daryl by hundreds of miles and an ocean still to come. The exhilaration of the morning mixed uneasily with the hollow space his absence left.

As the plane droned northward, my thoughts drifted to Rothsay where the wedding that should have been. While Phyllis and I were somewhere over Missouri farmland, over 200 friends and relatives had gathered at Hamar Lutheran Church. The organist played the processional we had chosen. The flowers were arranged with loving care. Reverend Maynard Stokka delivered the wedding sermon just as he had prepared, even though there was no bride or groom to receive it.

My parents and Daryl's parents stood in the reception line without us—my grandmother, Mrs. Haldor Hanson, and Daryl's grandparents, Mr. and Mrs. Walter Fabian, standing beside them. They greeted each guest who came through the line, offering smiles and explanations in our place. It was the wedding that happened without us—*heartbreaking, surreal, and touching all at once.*

Four hours later, the plane landed at Fergus Falls Municipal Airport. Darkness had settled over the October evening. As I walked toward my Chevy Malibu, a single sheet of paper caught my eye, flapping slightly in the cool wind. A note taped to the window read: "*Come to the Hamar Church. Your friends and family are waiting for you!*"

My heart leapt—and sank—at the same time. After the chaos, the travel, the tears, airsickness and emotionally spent, a reception was the last place I felt able to go. And yet, I knew I had to. They had all come for us. Somehow, I had to show up—for Daryl, for our families, and for the love that had carried us through an unforgettable, impossible day.

By 10 p.m., breathless and dazed, I walked into the room at Hamar Church. Laughter, clinking glasses, and warm congratulations surrounded me—but my groom was thousands of miles away, already en route to Germany. I smiled through tears, hugged relatives, and tried to absorb the joy that had been prepared for us. Singly, I cut the cake meant for two, sampled a slice of our three-tiered wedding cake topped with a cross and interlocking rings, and let the symbols of our Christian faith briefly bridge the gap between tradition and the chaos of the day. For one fleeting moment, everything felt ordinary, as if our wedding had followed the plan we had designed.

Yet the laughter around me only underscored the empty space where Daryl should have been. I returned home that night ALONE. The ceremony we had dreamed of—white dress with a short train, church bells ringing, vows before family—never happened. And yet, in its absence, something deeper forged: a marriage begun in chaos, sustained by faith, and carried forward by grace.

That night, as I lay in my childhood bed, curled beneath the quilt Grandma had sewn for me, the silence was deafening—no husband beside me, no honeymoon, but the echoes of vows spoken hours earlier in the ceremony we recreated. It wasn't at Hamar Lutheran Church, not with

Pastor Stokka, not with my wedding dress, not with the veil I'd rushed to replace, but in a Rolla, Missouri courtroom, 800 miles from home. The frantic race against time, fog and paperwork had led to this bittersweet moment. I was married, yes, but ALONE! It wasn't the ending I'd dreamed of—but it was the beginning of something stronger. A marriage forged not in tradition, but in fortitude, a bond tested by distance, circumstance, and time.

The next day was Sunday. Hushed as Sundays were in those years, stores were closed, streets quiet, families gathered at church or at home. That silence matched the emptiness I felt—a world at rest, while I was restless without my husband.

By Monday morning, life had returned to routine. Phyllis and I walked back into our classrooms in Fertile, Minnesota, as if nothing extraordinary had happened. Yet beneath the hum of spelling lessons and chalk dust, I carried the joy of vows spoken in Missouri and the ache of absence, knowing that even in our small community, our story was starting to take on a life of its own. My mother-in-law, the local newspaper reporter, would surely include the tale in area papers—but at that moment, I had no idea it would reach far beyond our town.

Days later, the whirlwind wedding story began traveling much farther than I imagined. As I sat at a kitchen table eating a bowl of Wheaties in the home of an elderly couple who rented me a room, the Associated Press called at 6:30 a.m., asking about our love story: *a determined bride who flew out of state to marry a GI before his unexpected deployment.* Newspapers across the country carried the headlines. Letters of congratulations poured in. In Rothsay, Minnesota, rumors buzzed. "Why would Donna fly to Missouri to marry her sweetheart?"

Later that week, I was shocked when listening to Paul Harvey, a legendary American broadcaster on the radio recounting our tale on *The Rest of the Story.* Daryl, relaxing in his barracks thousands of miles away, was also astonished to hear our private heartbreak—and triumph—shared on the National Forces Network.

As the whirlwind quieted and silence settled in, I saw what truly endured was not the race against time, against fog, against paperwork, against the chaos of the day, against the Army itself, but the promise we made. It wasn't lace or bells that made it happily ever after, but the vows whispered in a Missouri courthouse, fragile yet unbreakable. Like the fields of my childhood, our love would weather storms and seasons, yielding a harvest far richer than tradition alone could promise.

What I didn't yet know was that the real test of those vows was still ahead. Winter would come, and with it, our first Christmas apart—a season that would teach me how love stretches, adapts and survives across oceans.

Teaching Abroad and Building a Life

December arrived quietly, and with it came my first Christmas as a married woman living apart from my husband. In Fertile, Minnesota, I tried to keep my spirits lifted with small rituals. My second graders cut paper snowflakes for me with their crooked edges taped to the walls of my rented room. At Grandma's, the cousins teased me about mailing Daryl a fruitcake—"as if the Army doesn't have enough bricks already!" Their laughter helped, but beneath the holiday cheer, the ache of his absence lingered.

Across the ocean in Germany, Daryl found a pine branch, tin can, and sand, fashioning a makeshift Christmas tree for his barracks. He decorated it with scraps of ribbon and a few cards from home, a reminder that love can be nurtured even in the darkest of times. This holiday experience taught us how distance sharpens longing and devotion finds ways to bloom, even across oceans.

Looking back, that Christmas was just one small moment in a much larger story—one Daryl would later tell with a mix of humor and resignation. In 1966, he was stationed in Germany, working as the company clerk for a unit based near Dachua and Augsburg, Germany. His world was the orderly room—a narrow office that smelled of papers, and the bitter coffee that seemed to simmer on a hot plate all day long. Each morning he fed crisp sheets of paper into a heavy typewriter, slipping thin carbon paper between them so every report had copies. The keys struck the metal carriage with a sharp clack-clack-clack that echoed off the gray filing cabinets lining the walls. From his desk, he kept track of everyone in the company, including those who had requested a leave, were sick, and those promoted and transferred. Soldiers drifted in and out of his office all day, asking about pay, leave papers, or orders. The first sergeant's voice carried easily down the hall, and Daryl learned quickly that the orderly room was the nerve center of the whole company.

After three years of that rhythm—typewriter keys, stacks of forms, the steady shuffle of soldiers with their boots thudding on the worn floor, and paperwork—Daryl's discharge date finally arrived. He reported as instructed, ready to close this chapter of his life. But the Army, in its peculiar way, had other plans. The unit was holding a company picnic that day, and the people who needed to process his discharge were all flipping burgers instead of sitting behind their desks. He waited … And waited. By the time someone finally stamped his papers, his service had stretched three years and a day or two, thanks to a picnic! It wasn't the first time the Army had rearranged our plans. Three years earlier, his leave to marry me had been suddenly canceled, and he was sent to Germany instead. Yet, we learned to take Army plans one day at a time, knowing that patience was part of the journey.

Eight months later, when June arrived and school was out in Fertile, Minnesota, I boarded a plane in Fargo bound for Munich. Finally, the time had come for Daryl and me to enjoy our new life together. The plane had maintenance issues, and I missed my first flight. With no easy way to communicate with Daryl, he had no idea what had happened at home. The airline promised to call ahead, but the message never reached Daryl. He waited eight hours at the airport, scanning each arrival. When I finally walked through the gate the next day, his shoulders dropped in relief! We embraced, both exhausted, both grateful—two weary travelers reunited at last!

Once our exhaustion subsided, we turned our attention to the practical matter of building our life together. Our first home was government housing in Munich: a multi-story, concrete apartment-style building known as "the quarters." The units were fully furnished with standard-issue furniture, bedding, and kitchen items. We took this apartment as no other housing was available at his base, 35 miles away in Dachau. A few months later, we moved into the "penthouse" level of an apartment building—once a maid's quarters, now our little nest. The U.S. Army installation bordered on the preserved grounds of the former Dachau Concentration Camp, a stark reminder of history that lived just beyond our windows. Daily life went on, but the weight of that place was never far from my mind.

I contacted the Department of Defense school nearby, a small building on the other side of the camp's fence line. One teacher covered first grade and part of second. I worked with the rest of the students in second grade, and those in third and fourth grade as well. The principal taught fifth grade. Supplies were scarce, but I had a box of pencils, paper, and crayons shipped from home—small treasures that became lifelines in the classroom.

Most of my students spoke German. Many of their fathers were in Vietnam and their mothers were raising them alone in government housing. After school, I often played catch with them outside the complex. They left little gifts at my door—drawings, flowers, trinkets—tokens of affection that made me feel like family. Teaching them was more than a job; it was a bridge between cultures, a reminder that children everywhere crave connection and stability.

My days were full of children and lessons, but our evenings took on a different kind of warmth. Daryl's Army friends, whose families remained in the States, often joined us for supper. "Donna," he'd say gently, "let's practice what you're making tonight." He wanted me to feel confident before serving a table of hungry servicemen. I cooked stews, casseroles, roasts—simple meals, but hearty. The men laughed, swapped stories, and for a few hours, the loneliness of separation eased. Those evenings taught me that home isn't always a place; sometimes it's a table crowded with people who need one another. Those shared meals made Germany feel like home, but not even that sense of belonging could soften the news that came next.

In the two years we lived in Germany, only one phone call reached us from home. My grandfather, who had immigrated from Norway, had passed away at 85. He had suffered a stroke sixteen years earlier, leaving him paralyzed on the left side, unable to walk or speak. Grandma had cared for him faithfully all those years. He never had the chance to return to Norway, the land he left behind. The news came across the line with a hollow echo, reminding me how far away we were—the distance made my grief sharper and more unreal.

In the months that followed, we tried to balance the heaviness of that loss with the opportunities before us. One of the highlights of our time abroad was visiting Berlin. The city was still divided, its streets humming with tension and history. As we approached Checkpoint Charlie, the air felt heavy, as though every breath carried the weight of struggle. Our bus was stopped, and armed guards climbed aboard, their boots striking the steps with deliberate force as they moved down the aisle, inspecting papers and peering into faces. No one spoke. We sat rigid in our seats, suddenly aware of how thin the barrier was between ordinary travel and something far more serious. Outside, other guards stood watch, their eyes scanning each passerby. The Wall itself loomed nearby, stark and unyielding, a concrete scar cut straight through the city.

Crossing into East Berlin was like stepping into another world. The streets were quieter, the buildings more austere, and the shop windows sparse. I remember whispering to Daryl, "It feels like the color has been drained out." Even the air seemed subdued, as if joy itself had been rationed. Yet life persisted—children played in courtyards, women carried baskets from markets and men hurried to work. Their resilience left an imprint on me.

In West Berlin, the contrast was startling. Cafés spilled

onto sidewalks, neon signs glowed, and music drifted from open doors. The city pulsed with defiance, determined to live fully despite the shadow of division. Standing there, I felt the fragility of freedom, the way it could be hemmed in by walls and watchtowers, yet still found ways to sing. That visit didn't just show me history; it also showed me the world's complexity, and my small but growing place within it.

After that trip, we settled back into our routines, unaware of how quickly things would change again. At the beginning of the next school year, Daryl was transferred to Augsburg, Germany. Having taught in Dachau, I was eager to return to a classroom in Germany. On the first day of school, 39 children crowded into a classroom. The first grade teacher was overwhelmed. I was hired to help share the teaching load which made that first day a little more manageable. The year in Dachau had not only prepared me for the challenges of an energetic classroom, it had also deepened my confidence and confirmed that teaching in Germany was exactly where I was meant to be at that point in my life.

During this season, weekends and vacations became our time to explore. We drove our fastback Volkswagen across Germany, Austria, Switzerland, Spain, France, the Netherlands, Denmark, Norway, Sweden, and the United Kingdom. We camped under stars, skied in Garmish and Berchtesgaden, Germany and stood in awe of the Alps. Those travels stitched themselves into the fabric of our young marriage with shared discoveries and wonders.

As that school year progressed, our time in Germany with

Daryl as a company clerk and me as a first grade teacher was drawing to close. Daryl extended his service so I could finish the school year. This was another act of love, reminding me, "We're in this together." By June, we returned to the United States, settling in St. Paul, Minnesota. As we celebrated our return home with loved ones, I carried with me not only souvenirs and photographs, but lessons of fortitude, teaching, and partnership—strengths forged during our years abroad and ones that would guide us through every chapter that followed.

Epilogue

The years after Germany unfolded like a carefully stitched quilt—patches of classrooms, family, travel, and quiet moments of love, each one shaping the life Daryl and I were building together. Every challenge we met, every small victory, became a thread in the fabric of our shared journey.

I taught for eleven years before stepping away to raise our children. Those years at home were no pause but a different kind of teaching—lessons in patience, nurturing, and the quiet artistry of shaping lives. When I returned to the classroom, education had changed, and so had I. New methods, fresh challenges, and unexpected expectations greeted me, and I met them with the same tenacity I had learned in the fields of Rothsay.

Retirement in 2005 was not an ending but a transition. I continued teaching for two universities and consulting nationwide, sharing what decades of experience had taught me. In 2009, I shifted to online teaching, moving from Minnesota to Iowa to care for our daughter's twins while she practiced as a pediatrician. Teaching online opened another chapter, allowing me to balance family and vocation in ways I had never imagined. By 2016, I retired from online teaching, closing the formal chapter of my career.

The story of our later years—when our daughter moved to California, and Daryl and I returned to Minnesota to live above our son's garage as we faced the challenges of Parkinson's together—belongs to another book. But the foundation for that journey had already been laid. From the harvest fields of Minnesota to classrooms across the world, from the laughter of children at home to the quiet endurance of family life, my path has always been shaped by heritage, love, and the courage to begin again.

And in that courage, may all our lives—yours and ours—be shaped by love, resilience, and the courage to begin again, over and over, through every turn of life's journey.

Author's Note

From the wide-open fields of my childhood farm to the classrooms where I first taught, this memoir follows the early years that shaped my life—through lessons learned, challenges met, and the quiet perseverance that carried me forward. It is a story of heritage, hard work, and the courage to begin anew, again and again.

Yet life had more challenges ahead. When my husband was diagnosed with Parkinson's disease, we faced a new journey—one that tested our patience, deepened our love, and strengthened the resolve I had cultivated over a lifetime. This chapter of our lives is explored in my book, *Parkinson's Caregiver: Strategies That Sustain*, where I share practical strategies, faith, and inner fortitude that helped us navigate the realities of caregiving.

If this memoir reveals the roots of my life, *Parkinson's Caregiver* celebrates the branches—the ways love, determination, and adaptability continue to grow, even in the face of illness.

Thank you for walking beside me through these pages. My hope is that together, these books offer not only a glimpse into my journey, but also inspiration and encouragement for anyone navigating their own path of perseverance, family, and caregiving.

Acknowledgments

I want to express my deepest gratitude to my family, who are the backdrop to so many of my favorite memories. To my four grandchildren and their parents, thank you for the cherished trips we've taken together over the years. These shared experiences are etched in my heart.

This memoir is dedicated to you. I hope it fills the gap Jack once pointed out when, after reading the dedication in my first book, he asked, "Grandma, why didn't you dedicate this book to me?" Jack, this one is for you—and for all of us.

To my husband, Daryl: your humor, patience, and love have shaped every chapter of my life. You often teased, "I just asked you a yes or no question, and you gave me a story!" Even as we navigate Parkinson's together, your light has never dimmed. Your absence on our travels now is bittersweet, a reminder of the joy you brought to every journey. This book, born from our shared resilience, is as much yours as it is mine.

To my daughter, Cheri: thank you for believing in me and for being the best audience a mother could ask for. Your enthusiasm for my stories—from growing up on the farm before electricity to the wedding that almost wasn't—helped bring this memoir to life.

My deepest thanks to my dear friend, Trudi, who read every chapter as it unfolded and offered thoughtful, encouraging feedback. Her support cheered me on every step of the way.

My heartfelt gratitude goes to Carolyn. Though we met professionally years ago, she quickly became a lasting source of inspiration in both my work and my life. Her insight and wisdom shaped this memoir in ways I will always treasure.

My sincere thanks also go to Jane, a Reading Recovery colleague from years ago and cherished friend. Her keen eye for detail strengthened this manuscript in ways I deeply appreciate.

And finally, a special acknowledgment to Ellen, an artist and writer I met by chance at the Capp Community Center e-charger. Our bond—strengthened by shared experiences with Parkinson's in our families—gave me the encouragement I needed to turn my passion into reality.

About the Author

Donna Hauger grew up on a Minnesota farm, where the values of resilience, faith, and hard work shaped her earliest years. Those lessons carried her through school, and into a lifelong vocation as a teacher. She began her career in elementary education, later teaching abroad in Germany, and eventually returned to Minnesota to raise a family while continuing to teach and inspire students.

Her passion for education extended far beyond the classroom. Over the decades, she taught at universities, worked as a national education consultant, and embraced new opportunities in online teaching. She balanced her professional commitments with family life, including a move to Iowa in 2009 to care for her daughter's twins while continuing to teach online. She retired from university teaching in 2016, but her journey of resilience and service continued.

She is also the author of *Parkinson's Caregiver: Strategies That Sustain*, a book drawn from her experience supporting her husband after his diagnosis offering practical guidance and encouragement to caregivers.

Today, Donna Hauger reflects on a journey that began in the farm fields of Minnesota and carried her into classrooms across the world. Her writing offers readers not only a glimpse into her own story, but also inspiration to face life's challenges with courage and hope.

www.ingramcontent.com/pod-product-compliance
Lightning Source LLC
Chambersburg PA
CBHW031137130726
47988CB00006B/2407